FILLED WITH

Mercy

DAILY REFLECTIONS ON
THE ATONEMENT

DESERET
BOOK

Salt Lake City, Utah

Library of Congress Cataloging-in-Publication Data

Filled with mercy : daily reflections on the Atonement.
    pages cm
  Includes bibliographical references.
  ISBN 978-1-60907-974-1 (hardbound : alk. paper)
1. Atonement—The Church of Jesus Christ of Latter-day Saints. 2. Atonement—Quotations, maxims, etc. 3. Christian life—Mormon authors. 4. Devotional calendars—The Church of Jesus Christ of Latter-day Saints.
  BX8643.A85F55 2014
  232'.3—dc23   2014027373

Printed in Canada
Friesens, Manitoba, Canada

10 9 8 7 6 5 4 3 2 1

PUBLISHER'S PREFACE

The entire plan of salvation depends on the Atonement of Jesus Christ. There is no doctrine more hopeful or more significant, more extensive in its reach or more personal in its application. But our finite minds have a difficult time grasping this infinite offering.

Gaining a true understanding of the Atonement is the quest of a lifetime and beyond. But every journey is undertaken a single step at a time, and that is what this book is designed for. Each page is an invitation to ponder just one specific thought about the Atonement. Drawn from the writings of prophets and poets, leaders and lay members of the Church from throughout the Restoration, these pearls of insight will help enhance our understanding of what Jesus Christ did for us and why.

The selections appear as they did when first published; no attempt has been made to standardize minor stylistic issues such as scriptural citations or capitalization. Rather, the authors' original preferences have been left intact.

It is hoped that these quotations, drawn from a wide variety of sources, will strengthen the reader's appreciation for the Atonement and provide lasting evidence of the love and mercy of our Heavenly Father and His Son, Jesus Christ.

JANUARY

His precious blood he freely spilt;
His life he freely gave,
A sinless sacrifice for guilt,
A dying world to save.

—Eliza R. Snow

Every attempt to reflect upon the Atonement, to study it, to embrace it, to express appreciation for it, however small or feeble it may be, will kindle the fires of faith and work its miracle towards a more Christlike life. It is an inescapable consequence of so doing. We become like those things we habitually love and admire. And thus, as we study Christ's life and live his teachings, we become more like him.

—TAD R. CALLISTER

A great many people have an idea that when he was on the cross, and nails were driven into his hands and feet, that was his great suffering. His great suffering was before he ever was placed upon the cross. It was in the Garden of Gethsemane.

—JOSEPH F. SMITH

Unrefreshed by food or sleep, after the terrible events of that night and morning, while His pallid Face bore the blood-marks from the crown of thorns, His mangled Body was unable to bear the weight of the Cross. No wonder the pity of the women of Jerusalem was stirred. But ours is not pity, it is worship at the sight. For, underlying His Human Weakness was the Divine Strength which led Him to this voluntary self-surrender. . . . It was the Divine strength of His pity and love which issued in His Human weakness.

—ALFRED EDERSHEIM

The Atonement of Christ is nothing less than the answer to the great and terrible question that life inevitably poses: "Is this all there is?" If you are a saint, you know that this is a wicked world; if you are the most cynical and worldly unbeliever, you still know by experience that it is a vicious one. It seems that everything we want here is either destructive or trivial. . . .

But it doesn't have to be that way. That is just the point. The Atonement makes available the only kind of lasting life worth having.

—Hugh W. Nibley

Surely he hath borne our griefs,
and carried our sorrows:
yet we did esteem him stricken,
smitten of God, and afflicted.
But he was wounded for our transgressions,
he was bruised for our iniquities:
the chastisement of our peace was upon him;
and with his stripes we are healed.

—Isaiah 53:4–5

I've sometimes wondered if the phrase "love of God" means *our* love of God or *His* love of us. . . . My own experience has convinced me that it is impossible in all practicality to separate the two. When I feel His love for me I instantaneously am flooded with my love for Him and vice versa. We cannot have one without the other. No wonder it is always simply and profoundly stated "the love of God." Sometimes the scriptures even seem to indicate that Jesus Christ Himself is "the love of God." Of course, the Savior would be the physical representation, the incarnate expression of God's love for us, and our acceptance of Him and our profound gratitude for His atoning sacrifice would be the ultimate expression of *our* love for the Father! The love of God is the heart of Christianity, the centerpiece of the plan of salvation, and opening our hearts to receive and give it is our daily opportunity.

—Virginia H. Pearce

Can we, even in the depths of disease, tell Him anything at all about suffering? In ways we cannot comprehend, our sicknesses and infirmities were borne by Him even before they were borne by us. The very weight of our combined sins caused Him to descend below all. We have never been, nor will we be, in depths such as He has known. Thus His atonement made perfect His empathy and His mercy and His capacity to succor us, for which we can be everlastingly grateful as He tutors us in our trials. There was no ram in the thicket at Calvary to spare Him, this Friend of Abraham and Isaac.

—Neal A. Maxwell

Often the reason some people can't fully accept the blessings of the gospel is because the weight of the demand for perfection has driven them to despair. They mistakenly feel that in order for the Atonement to work in their lives, they must first become perfect through their own efforts. But anyone who could meet this requirement would not need the Atonement at all, for such a person would already be reconciled to God, having achieved the celestial standard of perfection on his or her own without needing Christ and his atonement—and this is not possible.

—STEPHEN E. ROBINSON

[It is] not so important to know upon which great stone the Master leaned in agonizing decision-prayers in the Garden of Gethsemane, as to know that he did in that area conclude to accept voluntarily crucifixion for our sakes. Not so needful to know on which hill his cross was planted nor in what tomb his body lay nor in which garden he met Mary, but that he did hang in voluntary physical and mental agony; that his lifeless, bloodless body did lie in the tomb into the third day as prophesied, and above all that he did emerge a resurrected perfected one—the first fruits of all men in resurrection and the author of the gospel which could give eternal life to obedient man.

—Spencer W. Kimball

If we want to know the Lord, ultimately we will have to give away all our sins. I'm not saying we can't know him until we've given them all away, but we need to be in that process if we want to meet him. We must trust in the Atonement. Our only real affirmation of the Atonement is our own repentance. Otherwise, we mock God.

—ANN N. MADSEN

In Hebrew the word translated into English as *atone* means "to cover." Jesus atones for our sins in that he forgives them and thereby covers them, as a cloth might cover a table. Through the blood of Christ, our stains are removed, erased, blotted out of the memory of the Omniscient One (see D&C 58:42). In addition, the Savior covers our sins in the sense that he pays the price, much as we might say to a friend at a restaurant, "I'll cover it."

In Aramaic and in Arabic the word translated into English as *atone* means "to embrace." Because of our sins, we are separated from our Holy Father, but through the mediation of Jesus we are welcomed, received, and embraced.

—ROBERT L. MILLET

The comforts we have, the peace we have, and, most important, the faith and knowledge of the things of God that we have, were bought with a terrible price by those who have gone before us. . . . It is because of our Redeemer's life and sacrifice that we are here. It is because of His sacrificial atonement that we and all of the sons and daughters of God will partake of the salvation of the Lord. . . . It is because of the sacrificial redemption wrought by the Savior of the world that the great plan of the eternal gospel is made available to us under which those who die in the Lord shall not taste of death but shall have the opportunity of going on to a celestial and eternal glory. In our own helplessness, He becomes our rescuer, saving us from damnation and bringing us to eternal life.

—GORDON B. HINCKLEY

A divine debt has been contracted by the children, and the Father demands recompense. He says to his children on the earth, who are in sin and transgression, it is impossible for you to pay this debt; I have prepared a sacrifice; I will send my Only Begotten Son to pay this divine debt. Do we understand why he should sacrifice his life? . . . Unless God provides a Savior to pay this debt it can never be paid. Can all the wisdom of the world devise means by which we can be redeemed, and returned to the presence of our Father and elder brother, and dwell with holy angels and celestial beings? No; it is beyond the power and wisdom of the inhabitants of the earth that now live, or that ever did or ever will live, to prepare or create a sacrifice that will pay this divine debt. But God provided it, and his Son paid it, and we, each and every one, can now receive the truth and be saved in the kingdom of God.

—Brigham Young

Death has come to be the universal heritage; it may claim its victim in infancy or youth, in the period of life's prime, or its summons may be deferred until the snows of age have gathered upon the hoary head; it may befall as the result of accident or disease, by violence, or as we say, through natural causes; but come it must, as Satan well knows; and in this knowledge is his present though but temporary triumph. But the purposes of God, as they ever have been and ever shall be, are infinitely superior to the deepest designs of men or devils; and the Satanic machinations to make death inevitable, perpetual and supreme were provided against even before the first man had been created in the flesh. The atonement to be wrought by Jesus the Christ was ordained to overcome death and to provide a means of ransom from the power of Satan.

—JAMES E. TALMAGE

The concept of trust becomes penetrating to my soul and almost beyond comprehension when I consider the trust the Son must have had in each of us that we would do our part. Having paid that awful price in our behalf, he trusted that it would not be in vain. And even though he knew that some would not repent, would not turn to him and accept the gift of the Atonement, still his trust in the Father's plan was sufficient to carry our Savior and Redeemer all the way through the Garden of Gethsemane to the cross, until at last he could say, "It is finished" (John 19:30).

—ARDETH GREENE KAPP

A true faith in Christ is more than just knowing about Him or even believing He is divine. It is knowing that His Atonement is real, that its purpose is to transform us, and that it will be available as long as that perfecting process takes. We have a Savior who covers us, a Redeemer who changes us, and a Good Shepherd who is willing to go in search of us again and again—continuously.

—BRAD WILCOX

Although our experiences cannot be compared to the Savior's suffering as he wrought the Atonement, that concept of Gethsemane speaks to my heart. We all face monumental periods in our lives when we turn to the Lord and pour out our souls, for the pain is too great for us to stand alone. Sharing our burdens with our Savior is part of the process of perfection.

—Elaine L. Jack

Essential to an understanding of the aspect of the atonement of Christ which enables men to attain unto eternal life is a realization that mortal man, while he lives on earth, is enlightened by the spirit of God and that he is also tempted by Satan; that every human being who lives beyond the age of accountability yields to some degree to the temptations of Satan. Jesus, who was the Son of God in the flesh, as well as in the spirit, was the only exception....

Men, in the exercise of their own free agency, having disqualified themselves for a place in the kingdom of God, are banished therefrom and cannot by their own unaided efforts return. If they are ever to return, atonement for their sins must be made by someone not himself banished: Jesus was that one.

—MARION G. ROMNEY

We are told . . . that the atonement must needs be infinite. Why did it need an infinite atonement? For the simple reason that a stream can never rise higher than its fountain; and man having assumed a fleshly body and become of the earth earthy, and through the violation of a law having cut himself off from his association with his Father, and become subject to death; in this condition, as the mortal life of man was short, and in and of himself he could have no hope of benefitting himself, or redeeming himself from his fallen condition, or of bringing himself back to the presence of his Father, some superior agency was needed to elevate him above his low and degraded position. This superior agency was the Son of God, who had not, as man had, violated a law of His Father, but was yet one with His Father, possessing His glory, His power, His authority, His dominion.

—JOHN TAYLOR

He took upon himself the sins of all who shall repent, and gave his life that all might live. He brought about the resurrection for all. Do you realize that the creation of this earth, and all the work of Jesus and the prophets since the very beginning, was for *you*—that you might have immortality and eternal life—just as much as for anyone else?

—ELDRED G. SMITH

The scriptures are full of images of Christ as water and of his atonement as the water of life. For me, the Atonement is that ocean wave at the seashore that makes everything smooth again. I like to carry that metaphor, that image, around with me in my pocket every day. It is an extremely useful item. Every once in a while I take it out and look at it—turn it over in my mind and notice things about it. I notice, for instance, that there's always plenty of water—always enough to fill the very deepest hole, cover the highest mound of sand, and make them level again. . . . I also notice that the water is always there as the years go by, unchanging, constant, and endless as eternity. . . . I notice, too, that the water leaves *everything* washed clean.

—Sally B. Palmer

No human encounter, no tragic loss, no spiritual failure is beyond the pale of his present knowledge and compassion. . . . And any theology which teaches that there were some thing[s] he did *not* suffer is [a] falsification of his life. He knew them all. Why? That he might succor, which is to say comfort and heal, this people. He knew the full nature of the human struggle.

—Truman G. Madsen

One would think it would be easy to embrace and have faith in the gift of the Atonement. But I fear that some Latter-day Saints know just enough about the gospel to feel guilty that they are not measuring up to some undefinable standard but not enough about the Atonement to feel the peace and strength it affords us. . . . Perhaps some of us don't know how to draw the power of the Atonement into our lives; others aren't willing to seek its blessings. And some don't ask because they don't feel worthy. It's quite the irony that the gospel of the great Jehovah, which contains the power to save every human being and to strengthen every soul, is sometimes interpreted in such a way that feelings of inadequacy result.

—SHERI DEW

Because the Savior has suffered anything and everything that we could ever feel or experience, He can help the weak to become stronger. He understands our pain and will walk with us even in our darkest hours.

We long for the ultimate blessing of the Atonement—to become one with Him, to be in His divine presence, to be called individually by name as He warmly welcomes us home with a radiant smile, beckoning us with open arms to be enfolded in His boundless love.

—James E. Faust

And lo, he shall suffer temptations,
and pain of body, hunger, thirst, and fatigue,
even more than man can suffer,
except it be unto death;
for behold, blood cometh from every pore,
so great shall be his anguish
for the wickedness and the abominations
of his people.

—Mosiah 3:7

God lives, and He does not live less though you have injustice and adversity and pain and unkindness and violence and betrayal. God is in His heaven. We chose to come to an unjust world and suffer. But God is God, and He loves us. His Son died for us. There is for each of us, because of who we are and who He is and who we are together, hope. There is hope.

—CARLFRED BRODERICK

When I was a child, I thought being able to forgive was like puberty—something that just happened to you. I was wrong. Forgiveness is a high-level spiritual skill that demands great effort, yet pays large peaceful rewards. It is one major way to understand the Atonement. Never have I felt the Atonement more personally than when I worked for years to forgive someone who had wounded me to my very core. During that period of my life, few days went by that I didn't thank the Lord for the successful mission of his Only Begotten Son.

—CAROL L. CLARK

To the very end of his mortal life Jesus was demonstrating the grandeur of his spirit and the magnitude of his strength. He was not, even at this late hour, selfishly engrossed with his own sorrows or contemplating the impending pain. He was anxiously attending to the present and future needs of his beloved followers. He knew their own safety, individually and as a church, lay only in their unconditional love one for another. His entire energies seem to have been directed toward their needs, thus teaching by example what he was teaching by precept.

—HOWARD W. HUNTER

Behold the man!" said Pontius Pilate, Roman governor of Judea, as Jesus, platted with a crown of thorns and mockingly bedecked with a purple robe, stood before the mob who cried, "Crucify him, crucify him!"

Blinded by ignorance, bigotry, and jealousy, the crowd saw in the condemned man only a malefactor, a violator of traditional law, a blasphemer; one whom they madly and unjustly condemned to the cross. Only a comparatively small group of men and women beheld Him as He really is—the Son of God, the Redeemer of mankind!

—HEBER J. GRANT

The Atonement of Jesus Christ gives us reason every day to find happiness, even under the bleakest of circumstances. Often, this cheer comes from the realization that the Atonement offers us a second chance to change our lives through repentance. Sometimes, though, the Atonement cheers us because it helps us see that Christ has perfect compassion for us in our moments of trial and stress, those times when we're really doing things mostly right but find ourselves down and out nonetheless.

—TRENTON HICKMAN

If we were fortunate to own one of the few violins made by Stradivari, I doubt we would put it in the hands of a careless, naïve performer. No, we would put such an instrument into the hands of a virtuoso, whose talent would magnify and enrich the inherent qualities of the violin. Likewise, when we willingly and completely put our divinely inherited legacy from our Father in Heaven into the masterful hands of His Son, the very best of our instrumentation, as it were, is developed and enhanced.

I can think of no better hands in which we might place ourselves. He knows who we are and what we can become. He knows what we face and how we feel. Remember, He took upon Himself every condition that meets us in mortality so that He could understand how to succor us in our weakness and our distress.

—SANDRA ROGERS

FEBRUARY

—

'Tis sweet to sing the matchless love
Of Him who left his home above
And came to earth—oh, wondrous plan—
To suffer, bleed, and die for man!

—George A. Manwaring

[God] had the power to save, and He loved His Son, and He could have saved Him. . . . He saw that Son condemned; He saw Him drag the cross through the streets of Jerusalem and faint under its load. He saw the Son finally upon Calvary; He saw His body stretched out upon the wooden cross; He saw the cruel nails driven through hands and feet, and the blows that broke the skin, tore the flesh, and let out the life's blood of His Son. . . . Oh, in that moment when He might have saved His Son, I thank Him and praise Him that He did not fail us. . . . I rejoice that He did not interfere, and that His love for us made it possible for Him to endure to look upon the sufferings of His Son and give Him finally to us, our Saviour and our Redeemer.

—MELVIN J. BALLARD

The Savior's victory can compensate not only for our sins but also for our inadequacies; not only for our deliberate mistakes but also for our sins committed in ignorance, our errors of judgment, and our unavoidable imperfections. Our ultimate aspiration is more than being forgiven of sin—we seek to become holy, endowed affirmatively with Christlike attributes, at one with him, like him. Divine grace is the only source that can finally fulfill that aspiration, after all we can do.

—BRUCE C. HAFEN

Because we have such frequent opportunities to partake of the sacrament, at times our observance can feel routine. . . . Nonetheless, whenever possible, we should anticipate our active participation in this sacred process. I've found that if I select something in advance to ponder—a verse of scripture, a hymn, an important lesson from the past week—I am more engaged and receptive to spiritual promptings. At those times, the Atonement ceases to be merely a subject for mental contemplation and becomes a heartfelt experience. I feel my Savior's sacrifice, I feel specific remorse for anything in my life that separates me from him, and I feel deep resolve to show that I remember him in all that I do and say. I sincerely want to have that more contemplative and meaningful experience become for me the rule, rather than the exception, as I participate in the sacrament.

—KATHY D. PULLINS

Christ alone could perform the atoning sacrifice, because he alone lived a pure and sinless life yet understood sin in its fulness. He understood how it distorts all realities, destroys wisdom, and limits potential. . . . Because the Savior provided the escape from that pernicious process of distortion for the whole human race, we must draw upon that power if we want to stop the process in our own lives and for our posterity.

—STEPHEN R. COVEY

By faith in this atonement or plan of redemption, Abel offered to God a sacrifice that was accepted, which was the firstlings of the flock. Cain offered of the fruit of the ground, and was not accepted, because he could not do it in faith, he could have no faith, or could not exercise faith contrary to the plan of heaven. It must be shedding the blood of the Only Begotten to atone for man; for this was the plan of redemption; and without the shedding of blood was no remission; and as the sacrifice was instituted for a type, by which man was to discern the great Sacrifice which God had prepared; to offer a sacrifice contrary to that, no faith could be exercised, because redemption was not purchased in that way, nor the power of atonement instituted after that order.

—JOSEPH SMITH

Gethsemane, Calvary, the empty tomb—we cannot seriously reflect on the sacred and monumental events that occurred in these special locations without feeling a deep and overwhelming sense of gratitude and humility. With great reverence we read of what happened, but try as we might, we cannot begin to approach an understanding of how it happened. In this respect, the Atonement is incomprehensible. However, its effects in our lives need not be. We can and must understand how the Atonement acts as a constant force for good. We must recognize it as a gift from a loving Savior who will never give up on us.

—BRAD WILCOX

Grace, the divine gift of the Atonement, is a healing balm readily available to relieve our pain, a nourishing manna to assuage the hungers of our daily lives. In the arithmetic of the universe, how may grief, regret, or disappointment be accounted for when repentance does not apply or restitution is not possible? Only God's grace can balance the account.

—ELAINE SHAW SORENSON

Like His Father, Jesus exemplifies love perfectly. He so loved the Father and us that He meekly and submissively let His will be completely swallowed up in the will of the Father in order to accomplish the Atonement, including blessing billions and billions of us with the unmerited, universal resurrection. What He did is staggering even to contemplate. No wonder He can help us along. He knows the way.

—NEAL A. MAXWELL

The ability of man to be at one with God in both location and in likeness is possible only because the Savior first became at one with man in location, through his mortal birth, and at one with man in likeness, through his assumption of man's frailties—without ever abandoning his godlike character. Paul observed that the Savior became "*like* unto his brethren" (Hebrews 2:17; emphasis added). There was something in the Savior's descent that made possible man's ascent.

—TAD R. CALLISTER

In that [premortal] setting, we were in the very presence of and under the nurturing influence of divine love. In harmony with that love, Christ made the most momentous of decisions. In essence he offered himself to stand in for us, to diminish the cumulative anguish of the Father's family, preferring to suffer himself rather than witness our suffering.

—Truman G. Madsen

It is through meeting the challenges of our mortal journey that we become disciples of Christ. As we put our trust in him, he will bless us according to our faith. As we go through pains, sicknesses, afflictions, and temptations of every kind, our Savior will be there to succor us. He has paid the price through his atoning sacrifice to know us and to know how to help us. He knows how to deliver us safely back home. He is our Deliverer—our all!

—MARILYN S. BATEMAN

The errand of Jesus to earth was to bring his brethren and sisters back into the presence of the Father; he has done his part of the work, and it remains for us to do ours. There is not one thing that the Lord could do for the salvation of the human family that he has neglected to do; and it remains for the children of men to receive the truth or reject it; all that can be accomplished for their salvation, independent of them, has been accomplished in and by the Savior.

—BRIGHAM YOUNG

If there were no opposition to good, would there be any chance to exercise your agency or right to choose? To deny you that privilege would be to deny you the opportunity to grow in knowledge, experience, and power. God has given laws with penalties affixed so that man might be made afraid of sin and be guided into paths of truth and duty. (See Alma 42:20.)

And because there is this choice between good and evil, the Lord has provided a means for the return of those who go astray.

—HAROLD B. LEE

For God so loved the world,
that he gave his only begotten Son,
that whosoever believeth in him
should not perish,
but have everlasting life.

—JOHN 3:16

One day, when we seek, ask, and knock and the heavenly gate is opened, and we ask permission to enter, I think we will have to present something in ourselves recognizably heavenly in order to gain entrance. We have to practice at-one-ment here so that we will know how to act when we get to heaven.

—M. CATHERINE THOMAS

Perhaps the real jewel in Luke's magnificent treasure trove of writings is Luke 22, particularly his description of the Savior's agony in Gethsemane. This is not because of any sensationalistic quality (I think we actually recoil from such graphic descriptions of God's sufferings) but rather because of its unique details and singular lesson on what the Atonement cost—what price was paid. In fact, reading Luke 22 prompts us to cry out, "If a being who is all-powerful suffers that much, what hope is there for any of us? It looks like no one is immune from suffering!"

That is precisely the point. No one *is* immune from the trials, tribulations, and sufferings of mortality. But because Jesus did suffer so much, we don't have to.

—ANDREW C. SKINNER

Salvation is in Christ. It comes because of the infinite and eternal atonement which he wrought by the shedding of his blood. He is the Son of God, and he came into the world to ransom men from the temporal and spiritual death that came because of what we call the fall.

Through his goodness and grace all men will come forth from the grave, to be judged according to the deeds done in the flesh. Then those who have believed and obeyed his laws shall receive an inheritance of eternal life in his Father's kingdom. This glorious blessing is available because of his atoning sacrifice, and it is given to those who love and serve him with all their strength.

—JOSEPH FIELDING SMITH

It is in the goodness of God, not in the goodness of ourselves, that our hope of the Atonement lies. We must have faith in Christ—not only that he is *the* Savior, but that he is *our* Savior.

—CHIEKO OKAZAKI

Of all the impossible things that were ever done in the history of the world, of all the walk-on-water-difficult, heart-tearing things to face, surely the Savior's own sacrifice is unequaled. When faced with the reality of this sacrifice, Jesus himself pleaded with the Father that he would not have to go through it. Yet he did it. What power enabled him to accomplish it? It was his love.

—S. MICHAEL WILCOX

We are informed that we will not be held responsible for the sin of Adam, but that we will be held responsible for our own sins. The atonement of Jesus Christ removed from us the responsibility of atoning for the sin of father Adam, and he made it possible for us to live here upon the earth, and in due time, if we take advantage of our opportunities, we will be prepared to be resurrected from the dead when that time shall come.

—George Albert Smith

Rejection, sorrow for others' suffering, and his own physical pain were frequent companions in the Savior's mortal life. Jesus manifested his love toward those who desired his destruction in a different way than he did toward those who reverenced him; however, his words and behavior toward his enemies evidenced his sincere efforts to soften their hearts and invite repentance.

—CAMILLE FRONK OLSON

Christ's agony in the garden is unfathomable by the finite mind, both as to intensity and cause. . . . He struggled and groaned under a burden such as no other being who has lived on earth might even conceive as possible. It was not physical pain, nor mental anguish alone, that caused Him to suffer such torture as to produce an extrusion of blood from every pore; but a spiritual agony of soul such as only God was capable of experiencing. No other man, however great his powers of physical or mental endurance, could have suffered so; for his human organism would have succumbed, and syncope would have produced unconsciousness and welcome oblivion. In that hour of anguish Christ met and overcame all the horrors that Satan, "the prince of this world," could inflict.

—James E. Talmage

Christ came to do the will of the Father. We came to do the will of the Father. That is our mission. In the temple that principle is strongly taught. Does it not become manifest to us as we sit and ponder that the highest and holiest exemplar of this great quality, the capacity to do the will of the Father, in all history is the One who in Gethsemane said, "Not my will, but thine, be done"? (Luke 22:42). Do we not walk in his paths, even though they lead us through our own Gethsemanes, when we seek to do the will of our Father?

—Marion D. Hanks

Jesus Christ is my Savior, my Redeemer, my Light, my Advocate with the Father. . . . To come to an assurance that this is true is one of the best and sweetest of all feelings we can have in our hearts. Remember that He stands at the door knocking, hoping we'll open our heart to Him and allow Him and His influence to come in. Oh, if we could just trust Him completely! If only we could have even a little more understanding of what He went through for us!

—MARY ELLEN EDMUNDS

Jesus would provide a way for us to be resurrected and, by His shouldering our punishment and guilt, a way to be cleansed. However, those would not be the end of His gifts. He also took upon Himself our infirmities and sorrows. He provided a way for us to be consoled through every trial. He suffered alone so that we would never have to do the same. Through His Atonement all of us can be covered, helped, comforted, and ultimately embraced.

—BRAD WILCOX

The Atonement helps us to become perfect. It has a daily, weekly application. Sometimes we don't fully understand how to apply the Atonement; we can become confused, and then we get down on ourselves. We've been taught, "If I do my best, the Lord will make up the difference," but that statement may seem to imply that the Atonement works only at the end of this life. The Atonement is so much more—each day the power of the Atonement is there for us to cleanse our sins and help us become perfected in Christ.

—CAROL B. THOMAS

To [His disciples]—yes, to them all—He would that night be even a stumbling-block. And so had it been foretold of old (Zech. 13:7), that the Shepherd would be smitten, and the sheep scattered. Did this prophecy of His suffering, in its grand outlines, fill the mind of the Saviour as He went forth on His Passion? Such Old Testament thoughts were at any rate present with Him, when, not unconsciously nor of necessity, but as the Lamb of God, He went to the slaughter.

—ALFRED EDERSHEIM

When we withhold forgiveness from others, . . . we are in effect saying that the atonement alone was insufficient to pay for this sin. We are holding out for more. We are finding fault with the Lord's offering. . . . It is as if we are failing to forgive the Lord.

—JAMES L. FERRELL

MARCH

~

For us the blood of Christ was shed;
For us on Calvary's cross he bled,
And thus dispelled the awful gloom
That else were this creation's doom.

—JOHN NICHOLSON

The best man that ever lived on this earth only just made out to save himself through the grace of God. The best woman that ever lived on the earth has only made her escape from this world to a better one, with a full assurance of enjoying the first resurrection. It requires all the atonement of Christ, the mercy of the Father, the pity of angels and the grace of the Lord Jesus Christ to be with us always, and then to do the very best we possibly can, to get rid of this sin within us, so that we may escape from this world into the celestial kingdom.

—Brigham Young

We do not experience trials just to see if we will make it through. Each of us experiences the refiner's fire for one reason—to come to know the Refiner. We are not just tried; we are proven. Priceless lessons can be learned from the Master during times of adversity. It is in these moments of heartache that we come to know the Savior and more fully appreciate His atoning sacrifice. Lessons thus learned will prepare us to better endure what may follow and will sustain us through the darkest days of our lives. . . . Through the gift of the Atonement we will experience His healing power, if we but take the time to ask.

—EMILY FREEMAN

Not long ago I was driving from my home to a meeting. I was swirling with frustration and pain. Someone had attacked me—unjustly I thought—and for 45 minutes on the phone had itemized all my failings. . . . I gripped the steering wheel harder and harder. I laid out my case in my mind, I elaborated my defenses, I wept. And I felt my heart harden. I paused, and with that break in my inner turmoil, the thought came to me, "The Lord has already paid for what you are feeling. He has paid for the pain, the frustration, the angst. You can choose to carry it and play it out. But He has already atoned for those sins."

I nearly stopped the car in the middle of a very busy road. I had been taught.

—HEIDI S. SWINTON

Christ's personality . . . is such that throughout His existence, we see His love vigorously and constantly at work as he gladly used the opportunities at hand. In His first estate, He, as the virtuous volunteer, generously proffered Himself as our Savior. He has responded in love to the opportunities at hand, with the same love, humility, and submissiveness in His second estate, as He actually became our ransom to the Father, paying the price at Gethsemane and Calvary. Now, having marked and shown the path, He, as our risen and tutoring Lord, waits for us lovingly and personally with open arms to usher us into the third estate. Such is the constancy and kindness of Christ.

—NEAL A. MAXWELL

Under extreme duress, Jesus pleads with his Father to remove the bitter cup. This Son is the Well Beloved Son. He has never done anything wrong, never! He is perfect and has always sought to honor his Father, to do everything right and good and compassionate.

But the one thing the Father cannot now do for his perfect Son is the very thing his Well Beloved Son has suggested—remove the bitter cup. He must watch his Son go through all this agony and more. Perhaps it is no exaggeration to say that at that fateful moment in the Garden of Gethsemane almost two thousand years ago, two divine Beings suffered and sacrificed to bring about an eternity's worth of possibilities for you and me and billions upon billions of others.

—ANDREW C. SKINNER

And he shall go forth,
suffering pains and afflictions
and temptations of every kind;
and this that the word might be fulfilled
which saith he will take upon him
the pains and the sicknesses of his people.
And he will take upon him death,
that he may loose the bands of death
which bind his people;
and he will take upon him their infirmities,
that his bowels may be filled with mercy,
according to the flesh,
that he may know according to the flesh
how to succor his people
according to their infirmities.

—ALMA 7:11–12

Our Lord and Savior Jesus Christ, who marked the path and led the way, extends the invitation, "Come, follow me." . . . Can we tell him anything about struggle or suffering that he does not know and understand—anything about loneliness, about rejection, about abuse? Do you think he understands about sorrow? And though he was without sin himself, do you think he knows of the consequence of sin, when he voluntarily took upon himself the weight of all our sins and transgressions? If we choose to follow him, he will be with us even in the fiery furnace.

—ARDETH GREENE KAPP

The Fall and the Atonement are a package deal: the one brings the other into existence. I am not aware of any discussion of the Atonement in the Book of Mormon that is not accompanied, either directly or by implication, by a discussion of the Fall. We do not appreciate and treasure the medicine until we appreciate the seriousness of the malady. We cannot look earnestly and longingly to the Redeemer if we do not sense the need for redemption. Jesus came to earth to do more than offer sage advice. He is not merely a benevolent consultant or a spiritual adviser. He is our Savior. He came to save us.

—ROBERT L. MILLET

Man in his present condition is not equal with God. He cannot grasp the fullness of the plan of salvation. It reaches into eternity; and . . . it had its origin before the earth was framed. It was necessary that there should be, in the wisdom of God, an infinite atonement, that a Being pure and holy, such as the Son of God was, should come here and die, in order to make amends for the broken law.

—GEORGE Q. CANNON

Adam and Eve fell that they might have joy. But they didn't skip merrily out of Eden singing and wishing everyone a nice day. They walked in sorrow into a lonely world, where they earned their bread by the sweat of their brows and learned about joy in the midst of misery and pain. Can you imagine how Eve felt when she learned that her son Cain had taken the life of her son Abel and that God had banished Cain?

How could Mother Eve possibly have found joy in the middle of such affliction? She found it by letting the atonement of Christ heal her pain and sanctify her experience. Indeed, her experience with sin and misery played a crucial role in preparing her for the joy she ultimately found.

—MARIE K. HAFEN

The Eternal Father well understood the diverse natures and varied capacities of His spirit-offspring; and His infinite foreknowledge made plain to Him, even in the beginning, that in the school of life some of His children would succeed and others would fail; some would be faithful, others false; some would choose the good, others the evil. . . . He further foresaw that death would enter the world, and that the possession of bodies by His children would be of but brief individual duration. . . . It was necessary that a means of redemption be provided, whereby erring man might make amends, and by compliance with established law achieve salvation and eventual exaltation in the eternal worlds. The power of death was to be overcome, so that, though men would of necessity die, they would live anew, their spirits clothed with immortalized bodies over which death could not again prevail.

—JAMES E. TALMAGE

I suppose the greatest gift we have received from the Christ is the gift of himself. He lived among men. He revealed to us in word and deed the meaning of humility, meekness, mercy, love, and moral courage. In our doctrine, God sent his Only Begotten Son into the world because that son had already offered to come—to live and die for men, to give life and to give it "more abundantly" in those dimensions of life most worthy of man.

—LOWELL L. BENNION

We have a hope in Christ here and now. He died for our sins. Because of Him and His gospel, our sins are washed away in the waters of baptism; sin and iniquity are burned out of our souls as though by fire; and we become clean, we have a clear conscience, and we gain that peace which passeth understanding. . . .

I know that Jesus Christ is the Son of the living God and that He was crucified for the sins of the world. He is my friend, my Savior, my Lord, and my God.

—Spencer W. Kimball

Mortal life isn't fair, but it's real. When we understand things as they really are, though, real in the sense of divine destiny and eternal expectations, we can weather the unfairness. Because pain is part of the process of perfection, we can expect that we will experience pain of various kinds in this life. I've spoken a lot about the fact that in the eternities we can expect complete fairness and ultimate rewards for our righteous behavior. Paradoxically, we can still be happy, cheerful, pleasant, and joyful right now despite the pains. Our hope for a brighter day should never cloud the view of this day. We live in a beautiful world full of opportunities and challenges, promises and perils. The gospel of Jesus Christ and His Atonement hold the keys for happiness now and happiness eternally.

—NORA NYLUND

The Atonement not only benefits the sinner but also benefits those sinned against—that is, the victims. By forgiving "those who trespass against us" . . . the Atonement brings a measure of peace and comfort to those who have been innocently victimized by the sins of others. The basic source for the healing of the soul is the Atonement of Jesus Christ.

—JAMES E. FAUST

I have interviewed many who feel as if the blessings of the Atonement are meant for others and not them. . . . They don't feel like they qualify because their lives don't match what they consider to be the ideal. . . . The list of struggles seems endless. Obviously, many people live their lives far from the situations they planned and hoped for when they were children. This gives us all the more reason to turn to the Savior, whose message is not just "Come unto me," but "Come as you are." He doesn't say, "Go get your act together and then come back when you fit the mold." He says, in essence, "Let's start right where you are, and go from there."

—Brad Wilcox

At one end of the law is mercy in all its compassionate splendor, at the other is justice in all its stern reality. The Atonement is the one act in recorded history that demonstrated the maximum mercy, yet never robbed justice of one ounce of payment. The Atonement ran the full gamut of the law, end to end, mercy to justice.

—TAD R. CALLISTER

As the deadline [for preparing an important talk] approached, I experienced increased stress, and stress drives away the Spirit. I came to a point where I knew I could not do this alone; I desperately needed His help. I prayed for guidance, understanding, wisdom, and the enabling power of Jesus Christ. "Why is this so difficult?" I prayed.

With force and power these words came streaming into my mind: Because Satan does not want you to teach of the atonement of Jesus Christ. He knows that when we understand the enabling power of the Atonement, we will be changed; we will have strength beyond our natural abilities.

—CAROLYN J. RASMUS

I believe that the Almighty knew what He was going to do with this world before He made it. He knew what kind of spirits were going to occupy it, and what kind of work would have to be performed in order to save His sons and daughters who should come upon the earth. And in reading the history of the dealings of God with men, from the creation of the world to this dispensation, we see the Father has labored to bless His sons and daughters. He gave His only begotten Son to redeem the world—a sacrifice such as only God Himself could give.

—WILFORD WOODRUFF

The inevitability of sin means the inevitability of sinful habits and consequent alienation from God and His heaven. In His infinite love and compassion, however, God wills the reintegration of *every* individual into the Heavenly Family. The human freedom to sin thus collides with God's desire to exalt and bless. The problem of how to reconcile this tragic collision is the problem of atonement, by which we mean, full and harmonious reconciliation. . . .

The atonement of Jesus Christ, His agony in Gethsemane and His death on the cross, is the only action by which the wounds of sin and hurt that rend the world can be repaired.

—Terryl Givens and Fiona Givens

It is in moments of disappointment, heartache, and loneliness that we often make the decisions that forge our faith, mold our character, and fortify our convictions about the only source of strength and solace that satisfies. And that is Jesus Christ.... How can we expect to feel and taste the pure sweetness of the gospel of Jesus Christ, meaning specifically the power and peace of the atonement of Jesus Christ, unless there are times in our lives when we desperately need and seek that peace and power?

—SHERI DEW

I sense in a measure the meaning of His atonement. I cannot comprehend it all. It is so vast in its reach and yet so intimate in its effect that it defies comprehension. When all is said and done, when all of history is examined, when the deepest depths of the human mind have been explored, there is nothing so wonderful, so majestic, so tremendous as this act of grace when the Son of the Almighty, the prince of His Father's royal household, . . . gave His life in ignominy and pain so that all of the sons and daughters of God, of all generations of time, every one of whom must die, might walk again and live eternally.

—GORDON B. HINCKLEY

How fortunate we are to have the gospel of Jesus Christ as a guide, and the promise that if we will serve God we will be saved from destruction and, in fact, enjoy life to the full here and eternal life hereafter. Christ's whole mission was to make it possible for us to enjoy immortality and eternal life, and he gave us the plan by which we can accomplish this.

—N. Eldon Tanner

The greatest gift of the Atonement is that it is real and there for us regardless of the state of our testimony. Whether we believe it or not, it is true. The Savior lives. His Atonement allows us to try again, to repent, to have hope, and to live. He suffered, died, and rose again for us, regardless of where we are in our belief or doubt about that reality.

—ELAINE S. MARSHALL

There is not a word among those translated as "atonement" which does not plainly indicate the return to a former state or condition; one rejoins the family, returns to the Father, becomes united, reconciled, embracing and sitting down happily with others after a sad separation. We want to get back, but to do that, we must resist the alternative: being taken into the community of "the prince of this world."

—Hugh W. Nibley

Mercy claimeth the penitent,
and mercy cometh because of the atonement;
and the atonement bringeth to pass
the resurrection of the dead;
and the resurrection of the dead
bringeth back men into the presence of God;
and thus they are restored into his presence,
to be judged according to their works,
according to the law and justice.

—ALMA 42:23

Jesus, our Lord and Master, was the greatest example of all in following in obedience to his Father's commandments. His great agony in the Garden I presume has never been approached and cannot be matched by human man. . . . The Master did not want to endure what was before him even though he knew this was the major purpose of his coming to earth—but he did what his Father had asked, and because he did, he holds "all power . . . in heaven and in earth" (Matthew 28:18) and has, as Paul records, become "the author and finisher of our faith" (Hebrews 12:2), and as many as receive him become his sons and daughters.

—HARTMAN RECTOR JR.

While we may not be able to fully grasp how the Atonement operates as propitiation, that is, as payment of debt required by divine justice, we can understand the Lord's offering of mercy. That mercy becomes operative when we are blessed with the central epiphany of our spiritual life: although the Lord's understanding of my humanity, my failures, my pride, and my fear is thorough and perfect, so is His love and His optimism for my potential.

—JOHN R. ROSENBERG

What do you suppose it means to be "sorrowful . . . unto death?" Perhaps there are those listening today who have felt that same kind of soul-crushing sorrow. Try to imagine the weight of that sorrow, and notice that even Christ, who obviously had a strong and loving relationship with his Father in Heaven, sought additional strength from his earthly friends. Jesus pleads, "Tarry ye here, and watch with me." Has there ever been a time in your life when you have said to someone, "Don't leave me; stay with me"? We crave a loved one's presence when a spiritual night falls.

—Virginia U. Jensen

The Savior did not finish his work when he expired on the cross, when he cried out, "It is finished." He, in using those words, had no reference to his great mission to the earth, but merely to the agonies which he suffered. . . . His work was not completed; it was in fact only begun. If he had stopped here, instead of his being the Savior of the world, he, as well as all mankind, would have perished irredeemably, never to have come forth out of the grave; for it was designed from the beginning that he should be the first fruits of them that slept; it was part of the great plan that he should burst the bands of death and gain the victory over the grave. If, therefore, his mission had ceased when he gave up the ghost, the world would have slumbered in the dust in interminable death, never to have risen to live again.

—Joseph F. Smith

It would have been a marvelous experience to have been as closely associated with [Jesus] as were his disciples, but even they did not fully appreciate his mission. Though he explained his mission to them and told them that he would lay down his life for the salvation of mankind, that he would come forth again from the tomb on the third day, that he would take upon himself the sins of all mankind, it was difficult for his followers to understand these things....

Peter and others were permitted to witness the Master's transfiguration, and they had seen the wonderful miracles that he had performed; yet it was not until after his resurrection and his appearance and association with them prior to his ascension and after they had been endowed with the Holy Ghost on the day of Pentecost that they were prepared to proclaim to the world without fear that he was the Christ, the Son of the living God.

—JOSEPH ANDERSON

APRIL

⌒

Lives again our glorious King,
Where, O death, is now thy sting?
Once he died our souls to save,
Where thy victory, O grave?

—CHARLES WESLEY

With the approach of the Easter season, the world takes note of the greatest event known to mankind. The literalness of the death and burial and resurrection of Jesus Christ lifts him above the status of a great man or an inspired leader. To overcome death for all mankind, Jesus Christ had to be the Son of God and the Redeemer and Savior of the world.

—LOREN C. DUNN

There are times in our lives—there have been times in mine—when we see someone we love suffering, that if it were allowed, if God permitted it, we would take the suffering for them. I think most parents understand that. Most husbands and wives understand that. Sometimes children, in their love for each other and for parents, understand that. At times close friends understand that. However, it's not allowed us. I cannot take my wife or child's pain upon me. Through empathy I can try to share it, but I cannot transfer it and release them. But it was allowed once—during those moments when the Savior drank the bitter cup in Gethsemane, when he understood our suffering, our afflictions, our pains, the whole of human misery. I can almost hear a deeper prayer echoing beneath the vocalized one in Gethsemane, a transformation from "remove this cup," to "let me drink it for them."

—S. Michael Wilcox

Even when [Jesus] cried out to God using the most intimate of titles, "*Abba*, . . . all things are possible unto thee; take away this cup from me" (Mark 14:36), we knew God would not do this because Jesus' *Abba* is also our *Abba*. God could not take away Christ's bitter cup without causing bitter consequences for us. We knew God would stay the course because the cost of failure was too great. The prospect of losing us was totally unacceptable to Him, despite Jesus' plea. Even on Calvary, when Jesus was left all alone on the cross without the help of His Father, the Holy Spirit, or angels, we knew He would come through.

—BRAD WILCOX

What is the message of the gospel? Is it that we're weak, frail sinners? That Heavenly Father is disgusted and angry with us? That Jesus is sorry he died for us because it was a real waste of the Atonement? That all the angels have decided that giving us agency was a stupid thing to do? No! The message of the scriptures is that *nothing* can separate us from the love of Christ.

—CHIEKO OKAZAKI

We are all dependent upon Jesus Christ, upon his coming into the world to open the way whereby we might secure peace, happiness, and exaltation. And had he not made these exertions, we never could have been secured in these blessings and privileges which are guaranteed unto us in the Gospel, through the mediation of Jesus Christ, for he made the necessary exertions.

—Lorenzo Snow

The root cause of all human problems is estrangement from the Father, which began at the time of the Fall and continues each time any of us transgress the Father's laws. The root solution to this problem is found in the atonement of Christ. He atoned for both the fall of man through Adam's transgression and the fall of each individual through transgression, if we will receive his gift through obedience to the principles and ordinances of the gospel.

—Stephen R. Covey

Since the Paschal Supper Jesus had not tasted either food or drink. After the deep emotion of that Feast, with all of holiest institution which it included; after the anticipated betrayal of Judas, and after the farewell to His disciples, He had passed into Gethsemane. There for hours, alone—since His nearest disciples could not watch with Him even one hour—the deep waters had rolled up to His soul. He had drunk of them, immersed, almost perished in them. . . . From indignity to indignity, from torture to torture, had He been hurried all that livelong night, all that morning. All throughout He had borne Himself with a Divine Majesty, which had awakened alike the deeper feelings of Pilate and the infuriated hatred of the Jews.

—ALFRED EDERSHEIM

The sacrament is a memorial of Christ's life and death. When we think of his life we think of sacrifice. Not a moment of his existence on earth did Christ think more of himself than he did of his brethren and the people whom he came to save, always losing himself for the good of others, and finally giving his life for the redemption of mankind. When we partake of the sacrament in his presence we remember him, his life of sacrifice, and service; and we are inspired by that thought and memory. There is nothing won in this life without sacrifice. . . .

The partaking of the sacrament indicates also how communion with Christ may be secured. It cannot be obtained by Sunday righteousness and week-day indulgence. It implies that we will remember Christ always.

—David O. McKay

Christ came to reverse all the processes of death and not just to resurrect those who have been buried. The death *of* the body is not the same as the deaths *in* the body.

Such deaths occur in this world—in the blinding of the mind, in the hardening of the heart, in the numbing of the senses, in the thwarting of the spirit—and each is a form of slow suicide. For these and every other diminishment of our better selves, Christ's love and Christ's spirit are alone the full and lasting cure.

—Truman G. Madsen

Isn't it a marvelous thing to know that Jesus Christ knows how we feel and that He can succor us? There is no heartache that He has not felt, no sorrow that He has not experienced. We can lay our burdens at His feet and He will help us carry them. Some of the most sacred and meaningful moments of my life have been when, on my knees, with a heavy heart, I have poured out my soul to my Heavenly Father. The healing balm of those emotional and often painful moments was in knowing that the Savior knows and feels what I feel and helps me to carry my burdens. Sometimes I have prayed for certain trials to be taken away, and though that has not always happened, I have felt in every instance, that the trial has been softened and that I have been strengthened to handle it.

—JANINE T. CLARKE

It is our responsibility and glorious opportunity to bear constant testimony of Jesus the Christ. We must testify to the world of his godship, the actuality of his birth in the flesh of both divine and mortal parentage. He was selected to perform the essential mission of the restoration and redemption. This he did—he was crucified and rose from the grave, thus making it possible for every human being to be resurrected through this marvelous atonement of Jesus, saint and sinner alike. . . . To the question "What does Jesus mean to modern man?" I testify that he means everything.

—David B. Haight

There are those who have lost faith because of personal tragedies or troubles. Faced with problems akin to Job's, they have in effect accepted the invitation to curse God and die rather than to love God and gain the strength to endure their trials. There is, of course, in the promises of God no warrant that we will avoid the very experiences which we came here to undergo and through which we can learn reliance on the Lord. Jesus said, "In the world ye shall have tribulation: but be of good cheer; I have overcome the world." (John 16:33.) He had tribulation, and he overcame. And so may we, with his help.

—MARION D. HANKS

The mortal probation is provided as an opportunity for advancement; but so great are the difficulties and the dangers, so strong is the influence of evil in the world, and so weak is man in resistance thereto, that without the aid of a power above that of humanity no soul would find its way back to God from whom it came. The need of a Redeemer lies in the inability of man to raise himself from the temporal to the spiritual plane, from the lower kingdom to the higher.

—JAMES E. TALMAGE

Jesus . . . knew of his own impending fate. He spoke in parables of grain that had to die in order to bring forth fruit, and of a chosen son sent by his father into the family vineyard only to be killed as the father's servants before him had been killed. At times the burden seemed almost too heavy to bear. . . . His singleness of purpose and unwavering commitment to do the will of his Father carried him forward.

—HOWARD W. HUNTER

If in this life only
we have hope in Christ,
we are of all men most miserable.
But now is Christ risen from the dead,
and become the firstfruits of them that slept.
For since by man came death,
by man came also the resurrection of the dead.
For as in Adam all die,
even so in Christ shall all be made alive.

—1 CORINTHIANS 15:19–22

Jesus knew that the awful hour of His deepest humiliation had arrived—that from this moment till the utterance of that great cry with which He expired, nothing remained for Him on earth but the torture of physical pain and the poignancy of mental anguish. All that the human frame can tolerate of suffering was to be heaped upon His shrinking body; every misery that cruel and crushing insult can inflict was to weigh heavy on His soul; and in this torment of body and agony of soul even the high and radiant serenity of His divine spirit was to suffer a short but terrible eclipse. Pain in its acutest sting, shame in its most overwhelming brutality, all the burden of the sin and mystery of man's existence in its apostasy and fall—this was what He must now face in all its most inexplicable accumulation."

—FREDERIC FARRAR

Mortality exacts of every one of us more "penalties" than we are able to pay. We are subject to the consequences of our sins, our bad choices. We also make mistakes out of our weakness that aren't intentional sins but that still bear consequences. And we all know people who have suffered the consequences of the sins and mistakes made by others. Finally, many suffer innocently the effects of living in a world where things like tsunamis and hurricanes and typhus and smallpox happen. It doesn't seem fair. From our limited perspective, in fact, it isn't fair. But is this really as bad as it seems? What if we knew that Someone had paid in advance for all these difficulties? . . . What if, in turning us to heaven because we have nowhere else to go, our difficulties actually point the path to the salvation and exaltation we came to earth seeking in the first place? It's a different perspective, isn't it?

—EMILY WATTS

It is a very great blessing that in the providences of the Lord and in the revelations that have been given by our Father in heaven, we have the assurance that the spirit and the body, in due time, will be reunited, notwithstanding the unbelief that there is in the world today—and there certainly is great skepticism and unbelief in relation to this matter. But notwithstanding this, we have assurance through the revelations that have been given by the Lord our God, that that is the purpose of God, that the body and the spirit shall be eternally united and that there will come a time, through the blessing and mercy of God, when we will no more have sorrow but when we shall have conquered all of these things that are of a trying and distressing character, and shall stand up in the presence of the living God, filled with joy and peace and satisfaction.

—HEBER J. GRANT

Through his love and mercy, Jesus, the Good Shepherd, has called to each of us. To those who have sinned, he grants pardon. He rejoices in the salvation of man.

We can never fully repay our Savior for his sacrifice made to help us achieve salvation and exaltation. It would behoove each of us to search our hearts and lives and consider how good and gracious our Lord has been.

—Delbert L. Stapley

Forgiveness isn't just between two people. First and foremost, it's between you and the Lord. Why would that be? Think about the fact that the Savior came to earth in order to forgive everyone's sins. When He did that, He paid for the sins of the people who have hurt us, didn't He? So our holding out against those people and trying to punish them is really taking upon ourselves something that isn't our job. . . . That judgment belongs to the Savior because of what He did for all of us. That is part of His mission.

—Virginia H. Pearce

For those few moments in the eternal spectrum called mortality the Savior yielded to the mortal plight. . . . That he also had godly powers did not make his suffering any less excruciating, any less poignant, or any less real. To the contrary, it is for this very reason that his suffering was more, not less, than his mortal counterparts could experience. He took upon him infinite suffering, but chose to defend with only mortal faculties, with but one exception—his godhood was summoned to hold off unconsciousness and death (i.e., the twin relief mechanisms of man) that would otherwise over-power a mere mortal when he reached his threshold of pain. For the Savior, however, there would be no such relief. His divinity would be called upon, not to immunize him from pain, but to enlarge the receptacle that would hold it. He simply brought a larger cup to hold the bitter drink.

—TAD R. CALLISTER

God ... cannot lower the standard that we ultimately become perfect (see Matthew 5:48; 3 Nephi 12:48), but He can give us many opportunities to start again. ... We are all given the time we need to correct our mistakes. Perfection is our long-term goal, but for now our goal is progress in that direction—continuous progress that is possible only through the continuous Atonement.

—BRAD WILCOX

To be saved in [God's] presence is the greatest gift that can come to us, and to bring our family with us into the enjoyment of salvation will be the greatest achievement of our lives.

But we must understand that salvation is not a free gift. The offer is free indeed, through the atonement of the Savior. But its enjoyment must be earned, not with any halfhearted effort, but with wholesouled, undivided, concentrated application to a program of development which is called the gospel of the Lord Jesus Christ.

If we believe in immortality at all, we must also believe in God. And if we believe in him, we should accept the fact that it is possible for us to become like him. Actually, this is what God expects of us.

—MARK E. PETERSEN

Men cannot forgive their own sins; they cannot cleanse themselves from the consequences of their sins. Men can stop sinning and can do right in the future, and so far their acts are acceptable before the Lord and worthy of consideration. But who shall repair the wrongs they have done to themselves and to others, which it seems impossible for them to repair themselves? By the atonement of Jesus Christ the sins of the repentant shall be washed away; though they be crimson they shall be made white as wool.

—Joseph F. Smith

The symbolic significance of Jesus shedding his blood in Gethsemane has to do with the very place where it all happened. Gethsemane, the garden of the "oil press" on the Mount of Olives, is where olives were crushed to harvest their oil. Under extreme weight and pressure, the olives yielded their valuable fluid. Under extreme weight and pressure, Jesus bled from every pore. In Gethsemane, not only did Jesus become us but he became the olive. In the garden of the oil press, where olives were pressed out, Jesus himself was pressed out.

—ANDREW C. SKINNER

Each of us is like a powerhouse on a mighty river. The powerhouse has no power residing in itself; the potential power rests in the energy of the river. When that source of power flows through the generators of the power plant, power is transferred from the river to the power plant and sent out into the homes (lives) of others. The atonement of Christ is the power in the river. Faith is the generators that can harness that power. The power to achieve justification does not reside in us. We require the power of the atonement of Christ flowing into us. If no power is being generated, we do not—indeed, cannot—turn the generators by hand (justification by works); but rather, we make an effort to remove those things that have blocked the power from flowing into the generators (working righteousness as a result of faith).

—GERALD N. LUND

I know faith and hope are not a placebo meant to placate the questions and desires of our hearts. They are realities. My hope and my joy in life are based upon the atonement of our Savior and the restoration of the gospel in these days. I base my life on these truths; therefore, I have reason for my hope.

—ELAINE L. JACK

Jesus knew cognitively what He must do, but not experientially. He had never personally known the exquisite and exacting process of an atonement before. Thus, when the agony came in its fulness, it was so much, much worse than even He with his unique intellect had ever imagined! No wonder an angel appeared to strengthen him! (See Luke 22:43.)

The cumulative weight of all mortal sins—past, present, and future—pressed upon that perfect, sinless, and sensitive Soul! All our infirmities and sicknesses were somehow, too, a part of the awful arithmetic of the Atonement.

—NEAL A. MAXWELL

On the slope of the Mount of Olives was a garden area to which Jesus liked to retire for meditation and prayer. "Jesus ofttimes resorted thither with his disciples." (John 18:2.) The garden was appropriately named *Gat Shemen,* which in Hebrew means oil press. Just as the blood (juice) of the grape or olive is pressed and crushed by the heavy stone in the press, so the heavy burden of the sins of the world that was Jesus' to carry would press the blood out of the body of this Anointed One. In Gethsemane, among the olive trees, which were themselves symbolic of the people of Israel, was accomplished along with its consummation at Golgotha, the most selfless suffering in the history of humankind.

—D. Kelly Ogden

Was it known that man would fall? Yes. We are clearly told that it was understood that man should fall, and it was understood that the penalty of departing from the law would be death, death temporal. And there was a provision made for that. Man was not able to make that provision himself, and hence we are told that it needed the atonement of a God to accomplish this purpose; and the Son of God presented Himself to carry out that object. And when He presented Himself for this position He was accepted by His Father, just the same as any man who owes a debt, if he is not able to pay that obligation, and somebody steps forward and says, I will go security for him. If the persons to whom he is indebted are willing to take him as security they will receive the security's note or obligation to meet the debt. So Jesus offered Himself.

—JOHN TAYLOR

MAY

—

Prepare our minds that we may see
The beauties of thy grace,
Salvation purchased on that tree
For all who seek thy face.

—ANDREW DALRYMPLE

Christ's enabling power helps us feel happiness and cheer amid mortal gloom and doom. Misfortune and hardship lose their tragedy when viewed through the lens of the Atonement. The process could be explained this way: The more we know the Savior, the longer our view becomes. The more we see His truths, the more we feel His joy.

—CAMILLE FRONK OLSON

Here is an odd thing about the nature of mercy: by definition, mercy can only be mercy if we *don't* deserve it. For if we deserve something, then it becomes a matter of justice that we receive it. So it ceases to be a matter of mercy. Thus, in this sense at least, to give or to receive mercy is always somewhat unfair. But one of the great beauties of the gospel, some of the best news of all, is that Jesus Christ does not mind this unfairness. He is willing to suffer unfairly and compensate justice himself out of his own person in order to extend mercy to weaker beings like us. This willingness on his part to pay more than his fair share and to carry more than his fair load in order to grant mercy to others constitutes the grace of Christ.

—STEPHEN E. ROBINSON

We do not become perfect in one great act, just as we do not become irreversibly evil in one great act—or two. But painfully, slowly, it really is possible to push the inner circle toward the ideal. To trust the Savior's power in this matter is at the very heart of the gospel's purpose—to make bad men good and good men better.

—Bruce C. Hafen

No one can be admitted to any order of glory, in short, no soul can be saved until justice has been satisfied for violated law. Our belief in the universal application of the atonement implies no supposition that all mankind will be saved with like endowments of glory and power. In the kingdom of God there are numerous degrees or gradations provided for those who are worthy of them; in the house of our Father there are many mansions, into which only those who are prepared are admitted.

—James E. Talmage

Remember that there is no other way
nor means whereby man can be saved,
only through the atoning blood of Jesus Christ,
who shall come;
yea, remember that he cometh
to redeem the world.

—HELAMAN 5:9

The sacrament itself is an open proclamation of our faith in Christ. The very fact that we drink the cup and partake of the bread announces to everyone in the congregation: "I bear witness that Jesus is the atoning Christ who conquered death, both physically and spiritually." Each Sunday, therefore, is testimony Sunday, and every Sunday that we partake of those emblems, we bear our testimonies. Is not the most important testimony one can bear a declaration that Jesus truly is our Redeemer? The next time you take the sacrament, consciously think in your mind, "Today I bear my witness to everybody who sees me by this outward act that I have faith in the atoning sacrifice of Jesus."

—S. Michael Wilcox

Whenever the Lord revealed Himself to men in ancient days, and commanded them to offer sacrifice to Him, . . . it was done that they might look forward in faith to the time of His coming, and rely upon the power of that atonement for a remission of their sins. And this they have done, thousands who have gone before us, whose garments are spotless, and who are, like Job, waiting with an assurance like his, that they will see Him in the latter day upon the earth, even in their flesh.

—JOSEPH SMITH

I am a visual learner. If I can see something, I can remember it, and it's real to me. Christ always said, "Come unto me." But if I want to understand and know the Savior, I have to say to him, "Come unto me. Visit me in my house, in my space on earth." And if he would come and be right there close to me, I could say, "Lord, what wouldst thou have me do?" I have a good imagination, so I can see the Savior coming up the steps with the faulty rail, standing on my porch, and gently knocking on my door, wanting to come in and bring some peace and joy to my whirlwind. And I can see myself flinging that door open and saying, "Please, Savior, come in." That is how I remember Christ and his atonement in my everyday life. I visualize him being here with me.

—MARY B. KIRK

We may never understand nor comprehend in mortality how He accomplished what He did, but we must not fail to understand why He did what He did. All that He did was prompted by His unselfish, infinite love for us.

—EZRA TAFT BENSON

In the religion of atonement, we don't feel compelled to scapegoat in order to find justice and bring relief from guilt; the Savior fulfilled the demands of justice by suffering the effects of sin. Because we believe he paid for every sin, we do not desire to exact payment for whatever we have suffered. Instead, we are able to forgive freely, seeing even those who have wronged us with compassion. We let go of enmity, much as one whose boat has capsized might let go of a satchel of belongings that is dragging him or her underwater, might let it simply float away as obviously the lesser of two losses. For us, what Christ endured on our behalf is enough, and therefore we want for nothing.

—C. Terry Warner

As we increase our interactions with the Savior, as we really draw close to Him, He will become an increasing reality in our lives. And as we seek to understand the power of the Atonement, that it can be applied to our sins, our deficiencies, our pains, our frustrations, it can be the greatest reality in our lives.

—WENDY WATSON NELSON

At some point the multitudinous sins of countless ages were heaped upon the Savior, but his submissiveness was much more than a cold response to the demands of justice. This was not a nameless, passionless atonement performed by some detached, stoic being. Rather, it was an offering driven by infinite love. This was a personalized, not a mass atonement. Somehow, it may be that the sins of every soul were *individually* (as well as cumulatively) accounted for, suffered for, and redeemed for, all with a love unknown to man.

—TAD R. CALLISTER

Knowing about the Fall and its effects upon us is critical. Knowing of the forces in the world and within the human heart is vital. How I view the Fall will affect how I view Christ and the Atonement. If I understate or underestimate the Fall, I will not fully appreciate the breadth and depth and reach of our Lord's Atonement. . . .

Jesus is far more than a celestial cheerleader; he is my only hope for peace here and eternal life hereafter. Jesus is far more than a spiritual adviser; he is the sinless Son of Man who bids me to become as he is. Jesus is far more than a model of sane living; his is the power by which I may be reclaimed, regenerated, and renewed, changed into a new creature, a new creature alive in Christ.

—Robert L. Millet

Scientists tell us that the natural order of things in our universe is an irrevocable, steady movement toward decay: from life to death, from organization to chaos, from a condition or state of lesser degeneration to one of greater degeneration (a concept called entropy). This state of being is true for all kingdoms and creations—animals, plants, planets, stars, and other systems. Without Christ's atonement, human beings *and* the worlds on which they reside would be locked forever in the vise grip of death and dissolution. But with and through Christ's atonement, all things are made new. The process of decay is not only halted but reversed. Because of the Atonement, which includes events in Gethsemane as well as the universal resurrection, all things in the universe are empowered, renewed, and revitalized. Thus, Christ is the light and the *life* of the world.

—Andrew C. Skinner

The Atonement offers not just life but the chance to live "more abundantly" (John 10:10). It is not just about cleansing and consoling; it is also about transforming. My friend Omar Canals pointed out that while many Christians see the Atonement as a huge favor Christ did for us, Latter-day Saints also see it as a huge investment He made in us. Christ's Atonement is not just a golden ticket to get us into heaven. It is our opportunity to become heavenly—to become golden ourselves.

—BRAD WILCOX

Man was ordained in the beginning to become like Jesus Christ, to become conformed unto his image. As Jesus was born of woman, lived and grew to manhood, was put to death and raised from the dead to immortality and eternal life, so it was decreed in the beginning that man should be, and will be, through the atonement of Jesus, in spite of himself, resurrected from the dead. Death came upon us without the exercise of our agency; we had no hand in bringing it originally upon ourselves; it came because of the transgression of our first parents. Therefore, man, who had no hand in bringing death upon himself, shall have no hand in bringing again life unto himself; for as he dies in consequence of the sin of Adam, so shall he live again, whether he will or not, by the righteousness of Jesus Christ, and the power of his resurrection.

—Joseph F. Smith

Because [Jesus] knew the plan perfectly and knew us perfectly, he was willing to demonstrate through his perfect life the way we should go. . . . As we choose his way, we soon realize that it is not an easy path. His life and death and resurrection point us toward a life of sacrifice for others, of looking beyond ourselves to the needs of those around us. It is a life characterized by complete obedience.

—Ann N. Madsen

When our Savior in humility came upon earth, the people said, "Who are you, that you should claim to be the Son of God? We know your father; he is Joseph, the carpenter. We know your mother; she is Mary. We have Moses and Abraham for our prophets, and we have no need of a man like you to come and speak to us in the name of the Lord." . . . But He was the Son of God, and He did have the right to speak in the name of the Father. The truths He brought to the earth came from the Father; and though they nailed Him to the cross, though they placed upon His head the plaited crown of thorns, and put the mock scepter in His hands, though they spilled His blood with the cruel spear, yet the word that He delivered to them was the word of the Lord, and He was indeed the Son of God.

—GEORGE ALBERT SMITH

This plan [of salvation] was laid out in the beginning by our Heavenly Father. It gives us access to the rich but dangerous experiences of mortality with full assurance that we can still return to God. This plan required a perfect Redeemer to live a sinless life and then experience through the Atonement all the consequences of sin and mortality that we undergo here. In this way He could be our perfect Judge. He fully understands all our grievances against one another. He also fully understands the private pains out of which we injure one another. He fully empathizes with every one of us. In His omnipotence He is uniquely able to pay all our debts to one another, in part because there are no liens against Him.

—WENDY ULRICH

All of us, before we were born on this planet, sanctioned, upheld, and agreed to a plan. Not only that, we concurred in the selection of the Savior, who was "chosen and appointed" to implement the Father's plan, and whose participation was a matter of covenant. That covenant everlastingly ties him to the Father and to the Holy Ghost in a mutual pact of redemption.

—TRUMAN G. MADSEN

Not only did Jesus come as a universal gift, He came as an individual offering with a personal message to each one of us. For each one of us He died on Calvary and His blood will conditionally save us. Not as nations, communities or groups, but as individuals.

—HEBER J. GRANT

The story of Eden . . . assures us of the reality of an eternal God, who is literally our Father and who created the world. It brings into clear focus the purpose of this mortal life. . . . The promised Savior becomes a living reality. Our awareness of His atoning sacrifice increases the gratitude we feel for His absolute love. The story assures us that we may return to that selfsame Heavenly Father who sent us. On that return we can depend. Through the Savior's atonement and through our repentance and obedience, we will report on our joys and our sorrows, and move on to our own eternal life.

—BEVERLY CAMPBELL

As a young missionary, I often used a bridge to demonstrate how the Atonement worked. I would explain that a wide chasm of sin separates us from God and that without a bridge spanning that chasm, we could never return to the presence of God. Through His atoning sacrifice, Jesus Christ built just such a bridge, making it possible for us to return to live with Heavenly Father. However, with that merciful bridge in place, it is up to us to cross the bridge. If we do not, I explained, we will remain separated from God.

Though this analogy still seems largely accurate to me, as a bishop I came to believe an important addition is necessary: The Lord has not only built the bridge, but if we seek His aid, He will also help us cross the bridge. . . . Though the Atonement makes repentance possible, most of us seem to need help from the Lord to be able to fully repent and take advantage of the Savior's marvelous gift.

—ROBERT EATON

Our little finite afflictions are but as a drop in the ocean, compared with the infinite and unspeakable agony borne by him for our sakes because we were not able to bear it for ourselves.

—ORSON F. WHITNEY

Yea, even so he shall be led,
crucified, and slain,
the flesh becoming subject even unto death,
the will of the Son being swallowed up
in the will of the Father.
And thus God breaketh the bands of death,
having gained the victory over death;
giving the Son power to make intercession
for the children of men.

—Mosiah 15:7–8

That very character that was looked upon, not as the Savior, but as an outcast, who was crucified between two thieves and treated with scorn and derision, will be greeted by all men as the only Being through whom they can obtain salvation.

—BRIGHAM YOUNG

I bear testimony of this . . . truth: Jesus Christ "the good shepherd giveth his life for the sheep" (John 10:11). He set forth his gospel; he took upon himself our sins. By him, through him, because of him and his atoning sacrifice, we may receive eternal life and exaltation. I believe with all my heart that my Redeemer lives. He is the Son of God, the Redeemer of the world, the Savior of all his Father's children. I have heard his voice and recognize his call to each one of us: Come. Come all the way home.

—Heidi S. Swinton

The Atonement of Jesus Christ is multidimensional: it involves not only the payment of a debt but also elements of love and of service. A study of the Atonement that omitted any of these dimensions would necessarily be fragmentary; the doctrines of the gospel do not have much meaning in abstract theory standing separate and apart from people. Therefore, as the Atonement shows us, we must have love for one another and teach the importance of service.

—ROBERT J. MATTHEWS

It is because of Heavenly Father's gift of His Son that all men—past, present, and future—can return to live with Him who is the Father of our spirits. But to insure that that can happen, it was first necessary for Jesus to come to earth in the flesh to teach men by His example the correct way to live and then to willingly give up His life and, in some miraculous way, accept the burden for the sins of mankind.

—SPENCER W. KIMBALL

Every ordinance and covenant binds us to the Savior. It is through His example and pure and perfect life that we are strengthened and enabled. It is because of His infinite Atonement that we can repent and become pure and virtuous. *He* is the pure addition we need to be enabled to enter into the Father's presence once again. His Atonement is the basis for every temple ordinance.

—Elaine S. Dalton

The Fall was designed—complete with all the accompanying misery and pain—to ultimately bring us freedom and happiness. There is no shortcut to the celestial kingdom. Everyone who ends up there must pass through the lone and dreary world on the way. God knew the problems associated with a mortal probation, but He also knew that Jesus would be the solution to those problems. To that end Christ was anointed. Just as the Fall was necessary to overcome the blockade that stood between our premortal spirits and their eternal potential, the Atonement was necessary to overcome all effects of the Fall.

—Brad Wilcox

JUNE

~

He seized the keys of death and hell
And bruised the serpent's head;
He bid the prison doors unfold,
The grave yield up her dead.

—RICHARD ALLDRIDGE

From the terrible conflict in Gethsemane, Christ emerged a victor. Though in the dark tribulation of that fearful hour He had pleaded that the bitter cup be removed from His lips, the request, however oft repeated, was always conditional; the accomplishment of the Father's will was never lost sight of as the object of the Son's supreme desire. The further tragedy of the night, and the cruel inflictions that awaited Him on the morrow, to culminate in the frightful tortures of the cross, could not exceed the bitter anguish through which He had successfully passed.

—JAMES E. TALMAGE

Now, the inhabitants of Judah had an idea that if they could only put to death the Messiah, that that would end his mission and work on the earth. Vain hope of that generation as well as this! When they led Jesus to the cross, the very moment that spirit departed from that sorrowful tabernacle, it held the keys of the kingdom of God in all of its strength and power and glory the same as he had done while in the body. And while the body lay in the tomb, Jesus of Nazareth went and preached to the spirits in prison, and when his mission was ended there, his spirit returned again to his tabernacle. Did the Jews kill the principles he taught? No. He burst the bonds of death, he conquered the tomb, and came forth with an immortal body filled with glory and eternal life, holding all the powers and keys he held while in the flesh.

—WILFORD WOODRUFF

Within a span of fifty-eight years, Mormon fought in several major battles and witnessed the death of tens of thousands of his people! Yet he was filled not with hate and bitterness but with the pure love of Christ. . . . How did Mormon manage to keep his spiritual sensitivity while growing up in an environment of war? He must have been renewed by the Atonement, which can take away not only the pain of our sins but also the pain of things that happen to us over which we have no control.

—JOHN BYTHEWAY

God's ways are higher than man's ways. We, as his children, barely understand the minutia of the multiplication tables of human existence, let alone the calculus of the cosmos. God could tell us neither how he brought to pass the Creation nor how he made possible the reality of the Resurrection, because, in our present condition, we would not be able to understand it fully.

Besides, it is not important that we know the *how* of the Atonement and Resurrection—it is enough that we know the redemptive *reality* of the Atonement and Resurrection.

—NEAL A. MAXWELL

No one as He would know what Death was (not dying, which men dread, but Christ dreaded not); no one could taste its bitterness as He. His going into Death was His final conflict with Satan for man, and on his behalf. By submitting to it He took away the power of Death; He disarmed Death by burying his shaft in His own Heart. And beyond this lies the deep, unutterable mystery of Christ bearing the penalty due to our sin, bearing our death, bearing the penalty of the broken Law, the accumulated guilt of humanity, and the holy wrath of the Righteous Judge upon them.

—ALFRED EDERSHEIM

Will you, for a moment, see yourself standing before Christ's outstretched arms as He waits for you to "come unto Him" and be encircled in the arms of His love? It is here you will be healed, nourished, loved, enabled, strengthened, and made whole. We need to learn to let the Savior carry our burdens and to go to Him regularly to seek His enabling power.

—CAROLYN J. RASMUS

To every disciple of every dispensation, Gethsemane was and is the sweetest of victories. . . . That victory means everything to us as mortals. Because of it, every human being who seeks God's love receives not only that love but hope as well. Yet, to the Sinless One himself, a being of infinite goodness and perfect sensitivity, Gethsemane was the ultimate torture, the darkest hour, the starkest terror. His most extreme distress had little to do with the thought of physical death, even the hideous kind of death brought on by crucifixion. Rather, to that one being in all the universe who was personally and completely undeserving of the horrible, infinite punishments inflicted, Gethsemane was the bitterest anguish, the greatest contradiction, the gravest injustice, the bitterest of cups to drink. Yet, the will of the Father was that the bitter cup be swallowed—drained to its dregs. And drained it was, swallowed to the last drop by Christ.

—ANDREW C. SKINNER

Christ is, indeed, the Savior of my soul, the Savior of mankind. He has sacrificed His life for us that we might be saved; He has broken the bands of death, and has bid defiance to the grave, and bids us follow Him. He has come forth from death unto life again. He has declared Himself to be the way of salvation, the light and the life of the world, and I believe it with all my heart.

—JOSEPH F. SMITH

We know that on some level Jesus experienced the totality of mortal existence in Gethsemane. It's our faith that he experienced everything—absolutely everything. Sometimes we don't think through the implications of that belief. We talk in great generalities about the sins of all humankind, about the suffering of the entire human family. But we don't experience pain in generalities. We experience it individually. That means Jesus knows what it felt like when your mother died of cancer—how it was for your mother, how it still is for you. He knows what it felt like to lose the student-body election. He knows that moment when the brakes locked, and the car started to skid.

—Chieko Okazaki

I bear testimony that you cannot sink farther than the light and sweeping intelligence of Jesus Christ can reach. I bear testimony that as long as there is one spark of the will to repent and to reach, *he is there.* He did not just descend to your condition; he descended below it, "that he might be in all and through all things, the light of truth" (D&C 88:6).

—TRUMAN G. MADSEN

In Latter-day Saint doctrine, the Atonement of Christ is far from being a merely theological, philosophical, or psychological exercise. At-one-ment fulfills the measure of man's creation and is the culmination of the plan of salvation. As such, it requires more than our casual attention as we live out our days on earth.

—HUGH W. NIBLEY

All things shall work together for your good. Do you believe it? Have you really thought about his wonderful promise, given through the prophet Isaiah, that he will give you "beauty for ashes"? (See Isaiah 61:3.) Ponder that one for a minute. Think about ashes, about what is left over after the most horrific destruction has occurred. Then picture the Lord taking that devastation and turning it into something beautiful. That is the sure promise of the Atonement: that all our losses will be made up to us. When a foundation such as that is in place, nothing that can happen in mortality could ever shake us.

—EMILY WATTS

The absolute necessity of the Atonement as it stands would further appear by the confidence one feels that if milder means could have been made to answer as an Atonement, or if the satisfaction to justice could have been set aside, or if man's reconciliation with the divine order of things could have been brought about by an act of pure benevolence without other consideration, it undoubtedly would have been done; for it is inconceivable that either God's justice or his mercy would require or permit more suffering on the part of the Redeemer than was absolutely necessary to accomplish the end proposed. Any suffering beyond that which was absolutely necessary would be cruelty, pure and simple, and unthinkable in a God of perfect justice and mercy.

—B. H. Roberts

Behold, I am he who was prepared
from the foundation of the world
to redeem my people.
Behold, I am Jesus Christ....
In me shall all mankind have life,
and that eternally,
even they who shall believe on my name;
and they shall become my sons
and my daughters.

—ETHER 3:14

That the spirit of man passes triumphantly through the portals of death into everlasting life is one of the glorious messages given by Christ, our Redeemer. To him this earthly career is but a day and its closing but the setting of life's sun. Death, but a sleep, is followed by a glorious awakening in the morning of an eternal realm.

—David O. McKay

If we accept and live the gospel, we shall be made whole, we shall be glorified, we shall be that much further on in our eternal progression. What oppositions we shall then meet, what conditions for creation we shall then obtain, what new wholes we may rise to has not been revealed to us, and if it were we would not understand. But for the time being, if we have not a full understanding of divine or human love, we can be given the experience of it. We may have the supreme experience of it in contemplating the atonement and in trying to live to be worthy of the love that it shows to us.

—ARTHUR HENRY KING

Pray in the believing attitude and realize the power of the prayer of faith, that truly the Lord has promised that whatsoever you ask of him in righteousness, believing that you will receive, if you ask it in the name of the Savior and if it is right, you will receive it. . . .

As you pray in the name of the Savior, do it in the full realization of his divine role as Advocate and Mediator, and as the Holy One of Israel who atoned for your sins, who suffered, bled, and died for you that you might find life and freedom.

—STEPHEN R. COVEY

The Son of God . . . had the power to make worlds, to direct them. He came here as the Only Begotten Son to fulfill a mission, to be as a Lamb slain before the foundation of the world, to bring about salvation to all mankind. By giving His life He opened the door to resurrection and taught the way by which we could gain eternal life, which means to go back into the presence of the Father and the Son. That was who Jesus was in all His grandeur.

—HAROLD B. LEE

Although one can meet the demands of justice by suffering for his own sins, such suffering will not change him. Just as a criminal can pay his debt to justice by doing time in prison and walk out unreformed, suffering alone does not guarantee change. . . . Lasting change, here and hereafter, comes only through Christ.

—Brad Wilcox

The Latter-day Saints believe in the Gospel of the Son of God, simply because it is true. They believe in baptism for the remission of sins, personal and by proxy; they believe that Jesus is the Savior of the world; they believe that all who attain to any glory whatever, in any kingdom, will do so because Jesus has purchased it by his atonement.

—BRIGHAM YOUNG

The miracle of the empty tomb and the subsequent appearances of the risen Lord stand as powerful reminders that the atoning mission of Jesus Christ was not limited to His suffering and death for our sins. As expressed by the Book of Mormon prophet Jacob, the goodness of God is manifest in His preparing a way to overcome the awful monsters of death and hell, which are physical and spiritual death (see 2 Nephi 9:10). Only by overcoming both of these obstacles through the Redemption and the Resurrection can God's children truly become "one" with Him again.

—ERIC D. HUNTSMAN

We are given the opportunity, any time we choose, to make a life change. That opportunity comes from Christ through the Atonement. If we turn to the Savior and seek His counsel, we too can be healed and given the chance to live again. This healing requires giving our whole heart to follow the counsel of the Lord.

—EMILY FREEMAN

I know that Jesus Christ is the Redeemer of the world, that he came into the world to take upon him the transgression of every soul who would repent; and that we, through our repentance and our faith and our acceptance of the principles of the gospel, shall receive full salvation through the shedding of his blood and through the atonement which he brought to pass that we might receive these blessings. Moreover, I know that all men shall be redeemed from death, because men are not responsible for death, therefore Jesus Christ has redeemed them from death through the shedding of his blood. They shall rise in the resurrection, every man to receive his reward according to his works.

—JOSEPH FIELDING SMITH

On the very cross itself, who was [Jesus] concerned about? Look at those famous statements from the cross. One of the first concerned assigning his disciple John to care for his mother: "Woman, behold thy son! . . . Behold thy mother!" (John 19:26–27). "To day shalt thou be with me in paradise" (Luke 23:43) was directed to those crucified with him. "Father, forgive them; for they know not what they do" (Luke 23:34) showed his concern even for his very persecutors and tormentors. He forgave them in the very act. It is one thing to forgive when the sin is over and the initial pain is gone; it is another to forgive at the very moment you are sinned against. He was always turned outward. Always outward, outward, outward! In this there is a great lesson for us all. In our own times of grief, when we are troubled and need solace, we can look outward toward those who are also troubled and give them solace.

—S. Michael Wilcox

Having "good cheer" because of Christ's atoning victory over death and hell—over temptation,
tribulation, sin, suffering, sorrow, weaknesses,
inadequacies, and all the effects of the Fall—is
faith-inspired confidence in the future. Like knowing the end from the beginning, we can rest assured that God and goodness will ultimately prevail. That "good cheer" evokes "things will all work
out" optimism.

—Brent L. Top

His only Begotten Son in the flesh had to call the attention of his associates to the fact that with all his majesty and his royalty, he still must live like other men. And when the time came for him to die, and be hung upon the cross, and cruelly tortured by those of his own people, his own race, he did not become angry, he did not resent the unkindness....

The people of the world do not understand some of these things, and particularly, many men cannot understand how the Savior felt when in the agony of his soul, he cried to his Heavenly Father, not to condemn and destroy these who were taking his mortal life, but he said: " . . . Father, forgive them; for they know not what they do." (Luke 23:34.)

—GEORGE ALBERT SMITH

The Lord Jesus Christ himself is that consolation, that compensation, designed from the foundation of the world to comfort the human pain of fallenness, to compensate men and women for their earthly reductions and sacrifices. Only the Atonement, or more expressly the at-one-ment, of the Redeemer and the redeemed can heal the pain of the Fall. When we feel how much he loves us, we cannot help but love him. . . . His love is the consolation.

—M. Catherine Thomas

Although [Christ's] teachings and attributes have been of inestimable value to the human family, they must be considered as by-products of those things that really command our veneration and our worship—his atonement for our sins and his resurrection from the dead. Unfortunately, too many men have worshipped at the shrine of Christ's attributes and ethics but have denied the divinity of their Redeemer.

—Howard W. Hunter

If a person believes that he can be helped, *personally,* by the atonement of Jesus Christ, then his faith is energized and his charity is quickened. However, if through repeated transgression a person concludes that he has forfeited the right to be rescued from sin, the resulting despair undermines his faith and dilutes his charity. . . . In this manner, Satan drives a wedge between the shame-filled sinner and a merciful God—because shame cannot comprehend mercy.

—DAVID A. WHETTEN

Jesus Christ . . . came into the world with power to lay down His life and take it up again, the only Being sent from God to earth who possessed the power to lay down His life and take it up again. To no other soul under heaven has this power been given, and He demonstrated the resurrection from death to life by His own example, and has freely offered the same deliverance to all the sons and daughters of God that ever lived on earth or that will ever live from henceforth.

Christ has opened up to the world, through faith and obedience, this hope of everlasting life and exaltation in His glorious kingdom. Who else has taught such doctrines as this? Who else has exemplified this power and has done the deed?

—JOSEPH F. SMITH

JULY

He left his Father's courts on high,
With man to live, for man to die,
A world to purchase and to save
And seal a triumph o'er the grave.

—Eliza R. Snow

When Judas led the soldiers and the high priests to the Garden of Gethsemane and betrayed [Jesus] with a kiss, Jesus could have spoken a single word and leveled the entire city of Jerusalem. When the servant of the high priest stepped forward and slapped his face, Jesus could have lifted a finger and sent that man back to his original elements. When another man stepped forward and spit in his face, Jesus had only to blink and our entire solar system could have been annihilated. But he stood there, he endured, he suffered, he condescended.

—GERALD N. LUND

Christ's suffering in his final hours and on the cross are difficult to comprehend. He could have withdrawn, but he was able to look ahead with commitment. His love for his disciples contrasts sharply with the behavior of his detractors: his forgiveness, kindness, humility, and quiet majesty stand against a background of jeers, hollow triumphs, and cold-hearted hatred. Those final hours culminated a ministry marked by exceptional experiences: feeding the five thousand, raising Lazarus, quiet moments with close family and friends, a bitter march dragging his cross through the streets of Jerusalem. I think of those hours when my commitment lags; he was asked to do more than I will ever understand.

—Elaine L. Jack

When the Savior asked to have the cup removed, he demonstrated his comprehension of the situation. He knew intellectually what the cup contained or he would not have asked to have it taken from him. Both the option and the power to retreat, to withdraw, or to abandon the ordeal at any stage were readily available. Satan's final taunt, "If thou be the Son of God, come down from the cross" (Matthew 27:40), was not an idle suggestion, but a powerful reminder that he could!

In every sense of the term, his was a conscious, deliberate decision. He knew all that could be known (or that his Father desired him to know) in advance of the infinite suffering that would soon be his and his alone. His eyes were wide open when he tendered the most loving offer of all time: "Here am I, send me" (Abraham 3:27).

—TAD R. CALLISTER

The law of justice, which cares nothing for us personally, was not concerned with who suffered, only that the disrupted scales be balanced, consequences administered, and order restored. Jesus, who does care deeply for us personally, was willing to pay that penalty with His blood and thus bought our freedom.

—Brad Wilcox

Wherefore, redemption cometh
in and through the Holy Messiah;
for he is full of grace and truth.
Behold, he offereth himself a sacrifice for sin,
to answer the ends of the law,
unto all those who have a broken heart
and a contrite spirit;
and unto none else
can the ends of the law be answered.

—2 NEPHI 2:6–7

The Lord has determined in His heart that He will try us until He knows what He can do with us. He tried His Son Jesus. . . . Before He [the Savior] came upon earth the Father had watched His course and knew that He could depend upon Him when the salvation of worlds should be at stake; and He was not disappointed.

—LORENZO SNOW

It is because of the power and scope of the Atonement that we have access to power to help us deal with our mortal weaknesses, our fears, our anxieties, and our lack of peace. We are connected to Someone who can and will make up the difference between who we are and who we want to be, between where we are and where we want to be—if we will come unto Him.

I, like you, have been blessed with many opportunities to exercise faith in Jesus Christ, experiment upon his word, and practice what I believe. Through those experiences I have come to know that because of the phenomenal act of atonement begun in the Garden of Gethsemane and completed on the cross at Calvary, there is power, peace, comfort, healing, and strength available to help us as we attempt to negotiate life's challenges.

—SHERI DEW

[Jesus] came into the world . . . clothed with double power—power to die, which He derived from His mother; and power to resist death, if He had so willed it, which He had inherited from His Father. Thus He had power both to live forever and also power to pass through the ordeal of death, that He might suffer it for all men, and come forth out of the grave to a newness of life—a resurrected being, to be clothed with immortality and eternal life, that all men might come forth out of the grave unto life eternal, if they will obey Him.

—JOSEPH F. SMITH

In Gethsemane, the contradictions that constitute the bitter cup are seen with crystal clarity. He who was the Son of the Highest descended below all things. He who was sinless was weighed down by the crushing sins of everyone else. He who was the light and the life of the world was surrounded by darkness and death. He who was sent to earth out of love and who was characterized as Love suffered the effects of enmity, or hatred, toward God. He who was the essence of loyalty was the object of betrayal and disloyalty. He who did nothing but good suffered evil. He who was the Righteous One was buffeted by the enemy of all righteousness. And from it all, he emerged victorious.

—ANDREW C. SKINNER

In the spirit of God-like mercy He prayed: *"Father, forgive them; for they know not what they do."* Let us not attempt to fix the limits of the Lord's mercy; that it would be extended to all who in any degree could justly come under the blessed boon thereof ought to be a sufficing fact. There is significance in the form in which this merciful benediction was expressed. Had the Lord said, "I forgive you," His gracious pardon may have been understood to be but a remission of the cruel offense against Himself as One tortured under unrighteous condemnation; but the invocation of the Father's forgiveness was a plea for those who had brought anguish and death to the Father's Well Beloved Son, the Savior and Redeemer of the world.

—JAMES E. TALMAGE

The wonder of the Atonement and the gospel covenant is that the sinless one offers to make a "great exchange": to take upon him our sins and to impute to us his righteousness (2 Corinthians 5:21). Our birth in the Spirit involves a "mighty change" in our nature, a change from worldliness to the pursuit of holiness (Mosiah 5:1–2).

—ROBERT L. MILLET

Since Jesus Christ alone paid the price for our sins, thus satisfying the claims of justice, we are bought by him and are therefore his. . . . Consequently, he alone sets the requirements necessary for us to be covered by his atoning sacrifice. Every person who is born into this fallen world is wholly dependent on him for salvation. We do not come to him on our terms, but on his terms, or we will never dwell in the kingdom of God.

—CAMILLE FRONK OLSON

Having bled at every pore, how red His raiment must have been in Gethsemane, how crimson that cloak!

No wonder, when Christ comes in power and glory, that He will come in reminding red attire (see D&C 133:48), signifying not only the winepress of wrath, but also to bring to our remembrance how He suffered for each of us in Gethsemane and on Calvary!

—Neal A. Maxwell

To reject the Lord and his love and his redeeming sacrifice is to deny the efficacy of God's love and his graciousness. All men are capable of mistakes, and have made some, but all of us too can have the cleansing forgiveness that comes with repentance and devotion.

—MARION D. HANKS

We partake of the sacrament for one most important reason, that we may always remember that sacred body that was offered up for our salvation, by which the ransom was paid and we were brought into communion with the Father and made heirs of salvation and joint heirs with Him who made the sacrifice.... So effectually and permanently does the Lord wish to impress the remembrance of that great sacrifice at Calvary on our memories that He permits us all to partake of the emblems—the bread and wine ... so that we may all remember Him.

—GEORGE Q. CANNON

The Atonement is an enabling power. As we turn to the Lord in prayer, He will make our weaknesses our strengths. We can trust in the Lord. You can trust the Lord with all your heart, and your faith will give you power beyond your own.

—ELAINE S. DALTON

Was His sacrifice necessary to enable us to rise into a life like His? . . . Yes. But the warm and over-whelming miracle is this: the more we approach Him and His likeness, the more we come to love as He loves, and the less we suffer needlessly.

—TRUMAN G. MADSEN

It was a merciful Jewish practice to give to those led to execution a draught of strong wine mixed with myrrh so as to deaden consciousness. . . . That draught was offered to Jesus when He reached Golgotha. But having tasted it, and ascertained its character and object, He would not drink it. . . . No man could take His Life from Him: He had power to lay it down, and to take it up again. Nor would He here yield to the ordinary weakness of our human nature; nor suffer and die as if it had been a necessity, not a voluntary self-surrender. He would meet Death, even in his sternest and fiercest mood, and conquer by submitting to the full. A lesson this also, though one difficult, to the Christian sufferer.

—ALFRED EDERSHEIM

[Jesus] died a propitiation for our sins to open the way for our resurrection, to point the way to our perfection of life, to show the way to exaltation. He died purposefully, voluntarily. His birth was humble, his life was perfect, his example was compelling; his death opened doors, and man was offered every good gift and blessing.

—SPENCER W. KIMBALL

Do we remember that at the great council in the heavens in which we participated as preexistent spiritual beings, he presented a plan in which he offered his life, and that he was willing to suffer death to atone for the sins that would come into the world? In doing this he would assure us of a resurrection from the dead, and he would make salvation possible for us, his brothers and sisters, and thus become our Savior.

Do we remember his intense agony and suffering in the Garden of Gethsemane, as he took upon himself the sins of mankind?

As we partake of the sacrament, do we remember that we enjoy membership in the restored church which bears his name; do we resolve that we will strive to demonstrate our appreciation by responding to calls and assignments made by our leaders; and do we commit ourselves to do everything within our power to help build up his church?

—HENRY D. TAYLOR

He suffered himself to be lifted up upon the cross that we might be lifted up, back to our Father, clothed with immortality and eternal life. And our part is easy, as simple in design as the Egyptian ankh. In faith, each of us takes the only thing we really have—our agency—and offers it back to him joyfully, voluntarily, and quietly.

—Virginia H. Pearce

When people think of the atonement, they most often think about how the Savior filled in the gaps for their *own* sins, which he surely did. That is, we are all sinners, and someone had to bridge for each of us the otherwise impassible chasm between us and eternal life that we have created through sin. So normally we think of the atonement as something that Christ has done for us—for ourselves. But . . . look at the atonement from a different angle—not from the perspective of how Christ has atoned for our *own* sins, but rather from the equally true perspective that he has atoned for the sins of *others*. And part of that atonement . . . is the idea that the Lord offers to those who have been harmed or potentially harmed by the sins of others the help and sustenance they need to be made whole.

—JAMES L. FERRELL

His peace will ease our suffering, bind up our broken hearts, blot out our hates, engender in our breasts a love of fellow men that will suffuse our souls with calm and happiness.

His message and the virtue of His atoning sacrifice reach out to the uttermost parts of the earth; they brood over the remotest seas. Wherever men go, there He may be reached. Where He is, there may the Holy Spirit be found also, with its fruit of "love, joy, peace, longsuffering, gentleness, goodness, faith" (Galatians 5:22).

—HEBER J. GRANT

For behold, I, God,
have suffered these things for all,
that they might not suffer if they would repent;
But if they would not repent
they must suffer even as I;
Which suffering caused myself,
even God, the greatest of all,
to tremble because of pain,
and to bleed at every pore,
and to suffer both body and spirit—
and would that I might not drink the bitter cup,
and shrink—
Nevertheless, glory be to the Father,
and I partook and finished my preparations
unto the children of men.

—D&C 19:16–19

We may not intrude too closely into this scene. It is shrouded in a halo and a mystery into which no footstep may penetrate. We, as we contemplate it, are like those disciples—our senses are confused, our perceptions are not clear. We can but enter into their amazement and sore distress. Half waking, half oppressed with an irresistible weight of troubled slumber, they only felt that they were dim witnesses of an unutterable agony, far deeper than anything which they could fathom, as it far transcended all that, even in our purest moments, we can pretend to understand.

—FREDERIC FARRAR

No one can learn of the amount of suffering Christ endured without wishing it might have been reduced. I used to think we could do that by not sinning, but of course that is impossible. I also thought maybe we could have eliminated the need for Christ's suffering by never leaving the premortal existence. Now I understand that even a refusal to leave would not have spared God and Christ their suffering because it would have meant a complete rejection of the Father's plan for our eternal progress and Christ's central role in it. Such rebellion may have even brought God and Jesus more suffering than they were to endure through the process of the Atonement....

God and Jesus knew that life would be far from predictable and full of influences beyond our control. They knew we would inevitably sin and that sin would mean suffering for them and for us. But we all still chose that suffering over the alternative.

—BRAD WILCOX

[In Nazareth,] I began to understand more fully that even though [Jesus] was divine, the Son of God, the Prince of Peace, the King of Glory, He was also mortal. He lived on the same earth we live on. He had to overcome the challenges of mortality even as you and I do. He had to discipline Himself to get up in the morning and do His chores. He had to study and learn. My love for Him knows no bounds.

Somehow He became more personal to me. I began to think of Him more when I faced the everyday challenges, knowing that He knew my feelings and would know exactly how to comfort me.

—MARJORIE PAY HINCKLEY

Adam became mortal; spiritual death came to him; and mortal death came to him. . . . In order for him to get back to the place whence he began, it was necessary that there should be an atonement for this disobedience.

Quite obviously, Adam could not retrace his steps; he could not un-eat. He was mortal. No matter how good any of his children might be, they, also mortal, had no more power than had he. So, to pay for the disobedience, it took a Being conceived by the Infinite, not subject to death as were Adam's posterity; someone to whom death was subject; someone born of woman but yet divine. He alone could make the sacrifice which would enable us to have our bodies and our spirits reunited in the due time of the Lord and then go back to the Father, thus reunited; and finally, body and spirit together, we might go on through all the eternities.

—J. REUBEN CLARK JR.

How the earthly father would love a child who would creep into his room with an angry, troubled face, and sit down at his feet, saying when asked what he wanted: "I feel so naughty, papa, and I want to get good!" Would he say to his child: "How dare you! Go away, and be good, and then come to me"? And shall we dare to think God would send us away if we came thus, and would not be pleased that we came, even if we were angry as Jonah? Would we not let all the tenderness of our nature flow forth upon such a child?

—GEORGE MACDONALD

As in all things, Jesus set the example for us.... In his great intercessory prayer he stated, "I have glorified thee on the earth: I have finished the work which thou gavest *me* to do" (John 17:4; emphasis added). If we are to use Christ as our guide through life, we too have to finish the work God has given *us* to do. I think Christ is trying to tell us simply and succinctly that complete joy will only be ours when our actions and aspirations match perfectly with God's plan for *us,* and not God's plan for somebody else.

—PATRICIA T. HOLLAND

While condemned in Jewish and Roman courts, Jesus was vindicated by the Father, who raised him from the dead. For the early disciples, the raising of Jesus was the Father's means of reversing the verdict of the human court. It was the key to understanding the humiliation, scandal, and apparent tragedy of the passion, and it constituted eternal and universal implications for humanity.

—RICHARD NEITZEL HOLZAPFEL

AUGUST

~

Come, Saints, and drop a tear or two
For him who groaned beneath your load;
He shed a thousand drops for you,
A thousand drops of precious blood.

—ISAAC WATTS

Do you remember the old object lessons we would sometimes see in classes on sin and repentance? You pound a nail into a board and pull it out. Sin is likened to the nail. You can pull it out with repentance, but the hole is there afterwards. I never felt comfortable looking at the hole still in the wood. I reject the whole idea. I think Christ's Atonement re-weaves the fibers of that board as if no nail was ever driven.

—S. Michael Wilcox

The Lord does not need to justify to us . . . why this setback or that disappointment, this challenge or that trial stands before us. The circumstance is a backdrop; hearkening to God's commands is about the feelings and response of the heart.

Will ours harden? Will we turn towards Him or turn away? Will we sustain and more importantly increase our trust in Him—come what may? . . . Will the Atonement of Jesus Christ become the strength and comfort that we need right now?

—HEIDI S. SWINTON

No member of this Church must ever forget the terrible price paid by our Redeemer, who gave his life that all men might live—the agony of Gethsemane, the bitter mockery of his trial, the vicious crown of thorns tearing at his flesh, the blood cry of the mob before Pilate, the lonely burden of his heavy walk along the way to Calvary, the terrifying pain as great nails pierced his hands and feet, the fevered torture of his body as he hung that tragic day, the Son of God, crying out, "Father, forgive them; for they know not what they do" (Luke 23:34)....

We cannot forget that. We must never forget it, for here our Savior, our Redeemer, the Son of God, gave himself a vicarious sacrifice for each of us.

—GORDON B. HINCKLEY

The reasons that Jesus performed miracles are probably as many and as diverse as the people whose lives were touched by them, not only the grateful recipients but those privileged to witness them. The overarching effect of the many miracles performed by Jesus, however, was to convince both recipients and witnesses of his true identity and the divine power he possesses over all things, both in heaven and on earth. All the things Jesus said and did seemed to have been to this end: to persuade men to accept his divinity and ultimately his atoning sacrifice.

—BRENT L. TOP

I have always looked upon the life of our Savior—who descended beneath all things that He might rise above all things—as an example for His followers. And yet it has always, in one sense of the word, seemed strange to me that the Son of God, the First Begotten in the eternal worlds of the Father, and the Only Begotten in the flesh, should have to descend to the earth and pass through what He did—born in a stable, cradled in a manger, persecuted, afflicted, scorned, a hiss and byeword to almost all the world, and especially to the inhabitants of Jerusalem and Judea. . . . And so all his life through, to the day of his death upon the cross. There is something about all this that appears sorrowful; but it seemed necessary for the Savior to descend below all things that he might ascend above all things.

—WILFORD WOODRUFF

We do not know, we cannot tell, no mortal mind can conceive the full import of what Christ did in Gethsemane.

We know he sweat great gouts of blood from every pore as he drained the dregs of that bitter cup his Father had given him.

We know he suffered, both body and spirit, more than it is possible for man to suffer, except it be unto death.

We know that in some way, incomprehensible to us, his suffering satisfied the demands of justice, ransomed penitent souls from the pains and penalties of sin, and made mercy available to those who believe in his holy name.

—BRUCE R. McCONKIE

Don't give up on anyone! Continue to minister, to care, to watch over others, even if they have not yet repented and responded fully to Christ and His Atonement. . . . We must continue to do what we can to help them come back so that Christ can heal them.

—MARY ELLEN EDMUNDS

Christ knows the full weight of our sins, for he carried it first. If our burden is not sin nor temptation, but illness or poverty or rejection, it's the same. He knows.

—HOWARD W. HUNTER

I can say to you in regard to Jesus and the atonement (it is so written, and I firmly believe it), that Christ has died for all. He has paid the full debt, whether you receive the gift or not. But if we continue to sin, to lie, steal, bear false witness, we must repent of and forsake that sin to have the full efficacy of the blood of Christ. Without this it will be of no effect; repentance must come, in order that the atonement may prove a benefit to us.

—BRIGHAM YOUNG

If sacrifice for others is the highest manifestation of love, then the Atonement of Jesus Christ is the grandest demonstration of love this world has ever known. The compelling, driving force behind his sacrifice was love, not duty or glory or honor or any other temporal reward. It was love in its purest, deepest, most enduring sense.

—TAD R. CALLISTER

Having worked out the Atonement, Jesus is everlastingly qualified to teach us of its significance and meaning for each of us. He was there. He was there for us. His experience reaches deeper than any of us presently can know. Perhaps that is why his love reaches miraculously to each of us and is the bridge that closes the distance between earth and heaven, providing us a way.

—ANN N. MADSEN

We cannot gain the abundant mind and heart of Christ on our own. We need the eternal, changing, healing power of the Atonement. We also need the perfect example of Christ's life. As we look towards that perfect life and rely on the Atonement to make up for the shortcomings we will inevitably detect, we can move closer to the abundant life in Christ. Only if we are constantly, deeply centered on Christ, can we make the changes that are necessary, for Christ is the great, eternal changing power.

—Stephen R. Covey

Now is my soul troubled; and what shall I say?
Father, save me from this hour:
but for this cause came I unto this hour.
Father, glorify thy name.
Then came there a voice from heaven, saying,
I have both glorified it,
and will glorify it again.

—JOHN 12:27–28

The more I understand God's wonderful plan of redemption, the more I realize that in the final judgment it will *not* be the unrepentant sinner begging Jesus, "Let me stay." No. He will probably be demanding, "Get me out of here!" Knowing Christ's character, I believe if anyone is going to be begging on that occasion, it will probably be Jesus begging the unrepentant sinner, "Please choose to stay. Please use my Atonement—not just to be cleansed so you qualify to stay, but to be changed so you *desire* to stay."

—BRAD WILCOX

Jesus passed through all the experiences of mortality just as you and I. He knew happiness, he experienced pain. He rejoiced as well as sorrowed with others. He knew friendship. He experienced, also, the sadness that comes through traitors and false accusers. He died a mortal death even as you will. Since Christ lived after death, so shall you, and so shall I.

—David O. McKay

The message of the Atonement is a message of joy. Our Savior knows our suffering. He took upon Himself our suffering that we might have joy. Joy is life. To have joy is to live fully. The meaning of the Resurrection in our own daily lives is that He lives! He lives, and because He lives, we live. This truth brings meaning, purpose, and joy to our lives. It gives us a reason to get up every morning (even in times of despair), to laugh with abandon, to embrace life. The good news of the gospel is for each of us to live. To live is to know joy in our own personal lives, every day, every now.

—ELAINE S. MARSHALL

But notwithstanding the transgression, by which man had cut himself off from an immediate intercourse with his Maker without a Mediator, it appears that the great and glorious plan of His redemption was previously provided; the sacrifice prepared; the atonement wrought out in the mind and purpose of God, even in the person of the Son, through whom man was now to look for acceptance and through whose merits he was now taught that he alone could find redemption, since the word had been pronounced, Unto dust thou shalt return.

—Joseph Smith

It was the purpose of the Father and the plan that men on earth should not forget what Adam taught. There was to be a Savior, and he was to do what his father intended—to be a lamb without blemish slain from before the foundation of the world—that is, the whole plan for the sacrifice of the Savior and for the redemption of men on earth was completed long before the earth was made....

He was to be despised and rejected and bruised for our iniquity. He was to bear our grief and carry our sorrows; he was himself to be a man of sorrow and acquainted with grief. He was to be brought as a lamb to the slaughter, yet he would open not his mouth, even as sheep brought to be sheared are dumb. He was to make his grave with the wicked and the rich. He was to be an offering for sin. (See Isaiah 53.)

—S. DILWORTH YOUNG

Today we should ask ourselves the question, in answer to what the Master asked of those in his day, "What think ye of Christ?" We ought to ask as we would say it today, "What think we of Christ?" and then make it a little more personal and ask, "What think I of Christ?" Do I think of him as the Redeemer of my soul? . . . Do I accept him as the Savior of this world? Am I true to my covenants, which in the waters of baptism, if I understood, meant that I would stand as a witness of him at all times, and in all things, and in all places, wherever I would be, even until death?

—HAROLD B. LEE

Because of the incomprehensible power of the Atonement not only is the earth redeemed and sanctified but it is destined to become the eternal abode and inheritance of all people who are similarly redeemed and sanctified by the very same atoning power of Jesus Christ. Thus, the Atonement connects people and planets in a seamless web of creation and redemption. In fact, every creature which fills the measure of its creation is likewise blessed by the power of the Atonement to inherit the kingdom of the Father's glory.

—ANDREW C. SKINNER

Now at last all that concerned the earthward aspect of His Mission—so far as it had to be done on the Cross—was ended. He had prayed for those who had nailed Him to it, in ignorance of what they did; He had given the comfort of assurance to the penitent, who had owned His Glory in His Humiliation; and He had made the last provision of love in regard to those nearest to Him. So to speak, the relations of His Humanity—that which touched His Human Nature in any direction—had been fully met. He had done with the Human aspect of His Work and with earth. And, appropriately, Nature seemed now to take sad farewell of Him, and mourned its departing Lord, Who, by His Personal connection with it, had once more lifted it from the abasement of the Fall into the region of the Divine, making it the dwelling-place, the vehicle for the manifestation, and the obedient messenger of the Divine.

—ALFRED EDERSHEIM

When we think of just our own world throughout history, the catalog of sins—murders, wars, immorality, selfishness, greed, idolatry, dishonesty—is so enormous that it is beyond comprehension. Think what kind of price was required to pay for all of that. Yet Christ took it all upon himself because of his perfect love for us. He who was holiest of all took all of humankind's vast storehouse of sin and evil upon himself.

—GERALD N. LUND

We knew we would make mistakes, be subject to the limitations of mortality, and suffer—but Jesus Christ promised that he would be our Savior. He would be born to a mortal mother, enter this world to teach us how to return to our Heavenly Parents, and, through the sacrifice of the Atonement, redeem us from our sins. We had no question that he would keep his promise, and we bound ourselves by covenant to accept him as our Savior.

—CHIEKO OKAZAKI

Jesus' daily mortal experiences and His ministry, to be sure, acquainted Him by observation with a sample of human sicknesses, grief, pains, sorrows, and infirmities which are "common to man" (1 Cor. 10:13). But the agonies of the Atonement were infinite and first-hand! Since not all human sorrow and pain is connected to sin, the full intensiveness of the Atonement involved bearing our pains, infirmities, and sicknesses, as well as our sins. Whatever our sufferings, we can safely cast our "care upon him; for he careth for [us]" (1 Pet. 5:7).

—NEAL A. MAXWELL

Jesus had not finished his work when his body was slain, neither did he finish it after his resurrection from the dead; although he had accomplished the purpose for which he then came to the earth, he had not fulfilled all his work. And when will he? Not until he has redeemed and saved every son and daughter of our father Adam that have been or ever will be born upon this earth to the end of time, except the sons of perdition. That is his mission.

—JOSEPH F. SMITH

When we tremble, when we bleed, when we suffer, either in body or in spirit, he understands. None is better qualified to see us through our mortal trials than he who "descended below all things" (D&C 88:6). If we truly understand what happened in the Garden of Gethsemane, we will have confidence in his sure promise found in Hebrews 13:5: "I will never leave thee, nor forsake thee." Just as my little grandson's mother did not immediately rush out and lift him up over the rocks, so our Savior does not remove our trials from us, though he clearly could. We are promised our trials will not be more than we can handle, but they cannot be less if we are to fulfill the measure of our creation.

—Virginia U. Jensen

Jesus Christ was the chosen and ordained Redeemer and Savior of mankind; to this exalted mission He had been set apart in the beginning, even before the earth was prepared as the abode of mankind. Unnumbered hosts who had never heard the gospel lived and died upon the earth before the birth of Jesus. Of those departed myriads many had passed their mortal probation with varying degrees of righteous observance of the law of God so far as it had been made known unto them, but had died in unblamable ignorance of the gospel; while other multitudes had lived and died as transgressors even against such moiety of God's law to man as they had learned and such as they had professed to obey. Death had claimed as its own all of these, both just and unjust. To them went the Christ, bearing the transcendently glorious tidings of redemption from the bondage of death, and of possible salvation from the effects of individual sin.

—James E. Talmage

The atonement of Jesus Christ has unfathomed intellectual aspects. And it is astonishing how much time we spend (I do not say waste) struggling to get it through our heads, to understand it. But a beginning of real understanding is to stand under it, to permit his power to reach *beyond* our depths so that Christ's life can grasp, shake, and transform our own. *That* is the point at which we are living or dying.

—TRUMAN G. MADSEN

We may not fully understand the theology of the Atonement nor completely comprehend the depth of God's love and mercy for us in giving us the free gift of life by the sacrifice of his Son. But I think we all yearn to feel the touch of grace in our lives, moments that capture the soul and hold it, a willing hostage, away from the assaults and demands of the unjust world in which we live.

—CAROL CORNWALL MADSEN

In its sweep and scope, the Atonement takes on the aspect of one of the grand constants in nature—omnipresent, unalterable, such as gravity or the speed of light. Just as for them, it is always there, easily forgotten, hard to explain, and hard to believe in without an explanation. But we are constantly exposed to its effects, whether we are aware of them or not, and to ignore it can be fatal. It is waiting at our disposal to draw us on.

—HUGH W. NIBLEY

I believe in Jesus Christ as the Son of God and the only begotten Son of the Father in the flesh; that he came into the world as the Redeemer, as the Savior; and through his death, through his ministry, the shedding of his blood, he has brought to pass redemption from death to all men, to all creatures—not alone to man, but to every living thing, and even to this earth itself, upon which we stand, for we are informed through the revelations that it too shall receive the resurrection and come forth to be crowned as a celestial body, and to be the abode of celestial beings eternally.

—JOSEPH FIELDING SMITH

SEPTEMBER

—

How infinite that wisdom,
The plan of holiness,
That made salvation perfect
And veiled the Lord in flesh.
—WILLIAM W. PHELPS

The mercy . . . freely offered through Christ's atonement, His gesture of supernal grace, cannot extend to the point of choosing on behalf of individuals. Repentance is therefore an ongoing process by which we repudiate unrighteous choices, acknowledging Christ's role in suffering the consequences of those sins on our behalf, and choosing afresh in accordance with purified desire. And so we go on choosing, again and again. The process continues—perhaps aeons into the future—until in perfect harmony with the laws that underlie the nature of happiness (and thus the nature of God), we have reached a sanctified condition that permits a perfect at-one-ment with God. God's desire to save is reconciled with the sanctity of human choice. Love and agency, justice and mercy, meet.

—TERRYL GIVENS AND FIONA GIVENS

Thus he shall bring salvation
to all those who shall believe on his name;
this being the intent of this last sacrifice,
to bring about the bowels of mercy,
which overpowereth justice,
and bringeth about means unto men
that they may have faith unto repentance.
And thus mercy can satisfy
the demands of justice,
and encircles them in the arms of safety.

—Alma 34:15–16

Through being the Son of God, living a sinless life, shedding his blood in the garden, sacrificing himself on the cross, and being resurrected, our Lord Jesus Christ made a perfect atonement available to all mankind. When we learn the truth and power of these facts, our hearts are filled with love for God our Father and his Son Jesus Christ, and we ever want to thank God for his plan and love in our behalf. It is the greatest story and message God can give to us—to let us know the reality of the Atonement and then how we can make it fully effective in our lives in order that we can return to live with him.

—N. Eldon Tanner

When the history of this world is finally written up with an eternal perspective, many events will vie as being worthy to be included. However, because of their significance to every person who has ever lived on this earth or who will ever live on it, the events of the last week of the Savior's life—from the Sunday morning of his triumphal entry into the city of Jerusalem to the Sunday morning of the resurrection—will undoubtedly be acclaimed as the greatest week in history. Without the events of that week, particularly those which took place in the Garden of Gethsemane and at the time of the resurrection, everything else is virtually meaningless.

—Daniel H. Ludlow

I know, as I know that I live, . . . that Jesus Christ is the Son of the Living God, the Redeemer of the world and that He came to this earth with a divine mission to die upon the cross as the Redeemer of mankind, atoning for the sins of the world. . . . I can bear testimony, from my own experience, that the oftener I read of the life and labors of our Lord and Savior Jesus Christ the greater are the joy, the peace, the happiness, the satisfaction that fill my soul in contemplating what he did.

—Heber J. Grant

The Atonement of Jesus Christ does not just provide a way to clean up messes; it provides the purpose and desire to avoid making more messes. The Atonement doesn't allow us to ignore our appetites or pretend they don't matter, but to educate and elevate them.

—BRAD WILCOX

Suppose at your command you could release your son from the exquisite pain that has caused him to cry, "Father, if thou be willing, remove this cup from me" (Luke 22:42). Which of us could resist such a request from a son who had never erred, never complained, never asked anything for himself—who all his life had honored and obeyed and served us, whose only thoughts were for others, and now in this moment of supreme agony pled for help, just this once, for himself? Would not our hearts have been bursting with compassion? Would not that cry of pathos, "My God, my God, why hast thou forsaken me," offered by the purest of all beings, the most obedient of all sons, so overpower us as to break our hearts and weaken our resolve? . . . Fortunately, even with his incomparable love for his Son, our Father in Heaven did not relent.

—TAD R. CALLISTER

The immense value of a mentor, a role model, quickly becomes apparent in any learning endeavor. Through our mentor's example, we are given a clear view of what is possible for us and what is required to achieve it.... In this sense, not only is Christ the great Mentor and Role Model because he obediently and diligently followed basic principles of God from the beginning, but because he alone can do for us what we can never do for ourselves, and thereby only he can show us the way to follow.

—CAMILLE FRONK OLSON

In that bitterest hour the dying Christ was alone, alone in most terrible reality. That the supreme sacrifice of the Son might be consummated in all its fulness, the Father seems to have withdrawn the support of His immediate Presence, leaving to the Savior of men the glory of complete victory over the forces of sin and death.

—James E. Talmage

This Jesus Christ, the Son of God, was once born in Bethlehem, crucified on Calvary, risen again from the dead, and having ascended to his Father and to our Father to lead captivity captive, and give gifts unto men, his name has become the only name under heaven through which man may be saved—receive everlasting life and exaltation. It is the only name by which man can get remission of sins, the gift of the Holy Spirit, and all its attendant blessings. It is the only name by which we may approach our Father in heaven and invoke His blessings—the only name by which we may control disease, and the very elements, by the power of His Spirit and the authority of His Priesthood.

—PARLEY P. PRATT

The fierceness of the wrath of Almighty God is a terrifying thing to contemplate. In Gethsemane Jesus took the full force of God's overwhelming and retributory punishment. Justice demanded it, and we, who are sinners, deserve it. According to the rules framing the universe, the full consequences of transgressed laws cannot be dismissed or overlooked. They must be borne by someone—the sinner or the substitute. Jesus was that substitute for all of us who will allow him to be so.

—ANDREW C. SKINNER

Christ in our lives is not meant to grieve us or weigh us down unto death because we have been imperfect. Through him we may be lifted up by accepting his gifts and his mercy and long-suffering. These blessings we must seek to keep in our minds always. . . . They who would follow him and be the manner of person he is will, as he did, lift up the repentant who suffer and sorrow for sin, and bless them with love and forgiveness.

—MARION D. HANKS

Because to be saved mankind must believe ... the doctrine that the Lord Omnipotent, the Preexisting One, shall take a mortal and then an immortal body in working out the infinite and eternal Atonement—Satan has labored incessantly to deny and stamp out the true message and messengers of the Messiah. Indeed, teaching the condescension of the great God proved costly to many.

—ROBERT L. MILLET

When we think of the resurrection of our Redeemer, I am reminded that the purpose of his life was to prepare us all, to make a path that we could all walk, that would bring us eternal happiness in his presence as well as in the presence of one another. He gave his life and testified by the shedding of his blood that he was a Son of God, and then . . . his appearance since that time has demonstrated beyond any possible doubt that he was what he claimed to be.

—GEORGE ALBERT SMITH

For each of us there will come a day when we wish we'd done things better, or when we realize that there is no way we can make everything right. If justice were demanded—if we had to pay a penalty for everything we've done wrong or for good things we failed to do—we simply could not do it. We could not pay the debt. But the debt has already been paid. Christ's death on the cross, "the great and last sacrifice," was to "bring about the bowels of mercy, which overpowereth justice; . . . mercy can satisfy the demands of justice." (Alma 34:15–16.)

For our sacrifice we are to offer "a broken heart and a contrite spirit"; to admit that we're sorry for our wrongdoings and that we want to do better. We acknowledge that we need Christ.

—Carolyn J. Rasmus

One day, no matter what reason we may have for unhappiness—whatever trials we may face, have faced, or are then facing—one day they will all come to an end. Right at the end of his agonies on the cross, Jesus said, "It is finished" (John 19:30). He certainly meant that his Father's will had completely been accomplished, but there is something more in those simple words. His *suffering* was also over. No man suffered more than he did, and if *he* came to a point in his life where he could say of his suffering, "It is finished," all of *us* will come to the point in our existence when we, too, will say, "It is finished." And it will be finished, no matter what it was. The tears will be wiped away. That end we may hope for. That end we may be assured of.

—S. MICHAEL WILCOX

It has been [more than] two thousand years since the wondrous occasion when death was conquered. We still do not know how the Savior was able to take upon himself and bear our transgressions, our foolishness, our grief, our sorrows, and our burdens. It was indefinable and unfathomable. It was almost unbearable. The indescribable agony was so great in Gethsemane that "his sweat was as it were great drops of blood falling down to the ground." (Luke 22:44.) The haunting cry on the cross, in a loud voice in his native Aramaic—"Eloi, Eloi, lama sabachthani? which is, being interpreted, My God, my God, why hast thou forsaken me?" (Mark 15:34)—gives but a mere glimpse of his suffering and humiliation. One cannot help wondering how many of those drops of precious blood each of us may be responsible for.

—JAMES E. FAUST

In the second [sacrament] prayer (the blessing of the water) we remember *his blood*. Why? Why blood? Is that not melodramatic? No. He is reminding us of more than blood from his side when someone threw or thrust a sword into him. More than the blood from the wounds in his hands and feet. He is reminding us of the blood that came from every pore of his body in those hours of the atonement, which to me are more inspiring than those on the cross. He is touching us with the power of recognition: that the blood he shed makes it possible for him to sanctify *our* blood.

—Truman G. Madsen

I've long believed that the closer we come to Christ, the more aware we are of what we yet lack in becoming like Him. At the same time, the closer we are, the more we can allow Him to help us become more perfect—more whole and complete, healed and pure. We become more able to have tears for His sorrows and pain at His grief—and to feel what causes Him sorrow and grief. We have more meekness in suffering and more praise for relief. We are increasingly aware of what He notices, what He feels, what He would have us do.

—MARY ELLEN EDMUNDS

The more we understand what really happened in the life of Jesus of Nazareth in Gethsemane and on Calvary, the better able we will be to understand the importance of sacrifice and selflessness in our lives.

—SPENCER W. KIMBALL

"Confessing Jesus" is not just believing in Him or experiencing a brief flirtation with spirituality. It is allowing our entire lives to be reshaped by Him. We accept the Atonement by faith, which includes repentance, covenants, and ordinances. Baptism and temple ordinances are not attempts to add to the finished work of Christ's sacrifice. These and other righteous works are extensions of our faith, by-products of our acceptance of Christ, and evidence of Christ working with, in, and through us. Faithfulness manifests our faith and strengthens it. Keeping covenants is not a way to prove ourselves worthy of grace, but rather a way to "grow in grace" (2 Peter 3:18).

—BRAD WILCOX

It behooveth the great Creator
that he suffereth himself
to become subject unto man in the flesh,
and die for all men,
that all men might become subject unto him.

—2 NEPHI 9:5

But one thing remained before the actual struggle, the veritable agony, began. He had to brace His body, to nerve His soul, to calm His spirit by prayer and solitude to meet that hour in which all that is evil in the Power of Evil should wreak its worst upon the Innocent and Holy. And He must face that hour alone: no human eye must witness, except through the twilight and shadow, the depth of His suffering. Yet He would have gladly shared their sympathy; it helped Him in this hour of darkness to feel that they were near, and that those were nearest who loved Him best.

—FREDERIC FARRAR

It is often in the valleys with our afflictions that we are truly humbled and better prepared to remember the gift of eternal life for which he paid the price—those times when we feel least worthy, least comfortable about carrying his holy name, and have a keener sense of our imperfections, those moments when the flesh is weak and our spirits suffer disappointment for our errors and our sins. We might feel a sense of withdrawal, a pulling away, a feeling of needing to set aside for a time at least that divine relationship with the Savior until we are more worthy. But at that very moment, even in our unworthiness, the offer is again given to us to accept the great gift of the Atonement—even before we change. When we feel the need to pull away, let us reach out to him. Instead of feeling the need to resist, let us submit to his will. Let us bend our will as well as our knees in humble supplication.

—ARDETH GREENE KAPP

Christ's Atonement is at the very core of God's plan. Without His dear, dear sacrifice, there would be no way home, no way to be together, no way to be like Him. He gave us all He had. Therefore, "how great is his joy" (D&C 18:13) when even one of us "gets it"—when we look up from the weed patch and turn our face to the Son.

—BRUCE C. HAFEN

When we come to the point where we understand the atoning sacrifice of the Master, we are approaching a spiritual maturity. I don't think spiritual maturity ever comes to us until we understand the true significance of the atoning sacrifice of the Master by which he gave his life that we might have life everlasting. When we understand the principle, we realize this is the greatest of love—that the Master laid down his life for us, that the grave will not be the end, but that we will live again.

—HOWARD W. HUNTER

The grace and faith by which man is saved are the gifts of God, having been purchased for him not by his own works, but by the blood of Christ. Had not these gifts been purchased for man, all exertions on his part would have been entirely unavailing and fruitless. Whatever course man might have pursued, he could not have atoned for one sin; it required the sacrifice of a sinless and pure Being in order to purchase the gifts of faith, repentance, and salvation for fallen man. Grace, Faith, Repentance, and Salvation, when considered in their origin, are not of man, neither by his works; man did not devise, originate, nor adopt them; superior Beings in Celestial abodes, provided these gifts, and revealed the conditions to man by which he might become a partaker of them. Therefore all boasting on the part of man is excluded. He is saved by a plan which his works did not originate—a plan of heaven, and not of earth.

—ORSON PRATT

Whether we underestimate our need for the Atonement or His willingness to forgive us when we repent, our Heavenly Father despairs when His people sometimes just don't get the Atonement. Whether we deny the need for the Atonement altogether, overlook our need for it individually, or underestimate the breadth and depth of its reach, our failure to recognize that God has "turned away [His] judgments because of [His] Son" (Alma 33:13) is highly offensive to the Lord.

—Robert Eaton

In an ultimate sense, of course, we cannot earn salvation by our wise choices or our good deeds. We do what we can, but the goal is far beyond us. Someone else must bridge the chasm. . . . Jesus reminded his disciples, "Ye have not chosen me, but I have chosen you" (John 15:16). We seek to follow the Savior, adhering to his teachings, emulating his virtues, enduring whatever burdens may be placed upon us, bearing his name, accepting his great sacrifice, and calling upon his grace. We then have to hope that he will reach out and draw us to him, making us more than we have made ourselves.

—Camilla Eyring Kimball

The infinite atonement is so vast and universal, but finally, it is so very personal! Mercifully, through the Atonement we can be forgiven and, very importantly, we can know that we have been forgiven—that final, joyous emancipation from error.

—NEAL A MAXWELL

OCTOBER

*I marvel that he would descend from his throne divine
To rescue a soul so rebellious and proud as mine,
That he should extend his great love unto such as I,
Sufficient to own, to redeem, and to justify.*

—CHARLES H. GABRIEL

We understood [in the premortal existence] what we don't see so clearly now: that God is a master, an expert, an absolute genius at turning trash into treasure, stupidity into wisdom, suffering into character, and sin (yes, even sin) into new life—*if,* and it is a big if—*if* we will let Him. *If we will catch hold of the vision of His redeeming plan and not let go, if* we will repent and have faith in the atonement of Christ, then God can not only save but also exalt us, even when we have been "the very vilest of sinners" (Mosiah 28:4).

—WENDY ULRICH

And this provision [the Atonement] applies not only to the living, but also to the dead, so that all men who have existed in all ages, who do exist now, or who will exist while the earth shall stand, may be placed upon the same footing and that all men may have the privilege, living or dead, of accepting the conditions of the great plan of redemption provided by the Father, through the Son, before the world was; and that the justice and mercy of God may be applied to every being, living or dead, that ever has existed, that does now exist, or that ever will exist.

—JOHN TAYLOR

I hope you know that even during the hardest moments of your life, when your powerlessness seems absolute and your isolation total, you are not alone. The Savior is with you, being with you as you endure the pain so that you can go on, healed and renewed. Your survival and even your triumph are assured through his atoning sacrifice and his love.

—CHIEKO OKAZAKI

There is a garden near some fruitful olive trees in Jerusalem. To it Jesus was wont to go. . . . On a given night anciently the power of his compassion, the power of his identifying imagination, the power of his sacrificial love began its awful work in his system. As he knelt under the ravages of all the forms of spiritual dying, he cried out for help. Even he? Yes! But was he not one who had moved "from grace to grace," one who had honored always the will of the Father? Did he not have sufficient strength to go through it? Thank the Lord for the message still in the record . . . that even he reached the limit.

—Truman G. Madsen

The victory of Christ over death and sin would be incomplete were its effects confined to the small minority who have heard, accepted, and lived the gospel of salvation in the flesh. Compliance with the laws and ordinances of the gospel is essential to salvation. Nowhere in scripture is a distinction made in this regard between the living and the dead. The dead are those who have lived in mortality upon earth; the living are mortals who yet shall pass through the ordained change which we call death. All are children of the same Father, all to be judged and rewarded or punished by the same unerring justice, with the same interposition of benign mercy. Christ's atoning sacrifice was offered, not alone for the few who lived upon the earth while He was in the flesh, nor for those who were born in mortality after His death, but for all inhabitants of earth then past, present, and future.

—JAMES E. TALMAGE

We accept without reservation the testimony of all of the evangelists contained in the New Testament with reference to the resurrection of the Redeemer of mankind. It is so plain that it seems to me that no thoughtful person can fail to comprehend it. The fact is that after the Savior was crucified and was laid in the tomb he came forth, and for forty days he associated with his disciples, he partook of fish and honeycomb with them, they felt the prints of the nails in his hands and the spear mark in his side. . . . Surely this is incontrovertible evidence and yet there are many of our Father's children who do not understand it.

—George Albert Smith

We know that even with the benefits of the Atonement fully operating in our lives, mortality still entails some suffering and some contradictions for each of us. Yet, because the Savior endured perfectly his staggering contradictions, we will be recompensed for our own faithful endurance of life's contradictions, injustices, and flat-out unfair circumstances. That is, through the Atonement, all of life's contradictions, all injustices, and all unfair circumstances will be made up to us, all unfair disadvantages will be made right in the eternal scheme of things. In an ironic twist, because of Christ's atonement, because of his supreme act of mercy which rescues us from the demands of justice, justice ultimately becomes our friend by making up to us for all of the things in life that weren't fair and right. All unfair circumstances and contradictions will be put right—if we remain faithful to the Savior.

—ANDREW C. SKINNER

Some things in life are temporary, and some are permanent. Our temporal life is temporary. Our trials are temporary. Our pain is temporary. Because of the Savior and his atonement, our mortality will become immortality, and we may dwell with God in a state of permanent, or "never-ending happiness" (Mosiah 2:41). . . . We know that the Lord will be victorious and that his victory will be permanent. That very thought should give us faith and hope.

—JOHN BYTHEWAY

If the end goal is just to be clean, start again, be healed, and go home, then why did we choose mortality, knowing full well we would get dirty, fail often, be broken, and lose our way? Clearly there had to be something more that drove us to enroll in this earthly school than getting to go home when the bell rings. We came because we had faith that through the Atonement each lesson we learned could make us better, stronger, and wiser. To that end, the Atonement is not just a helpful tool. It is an absolute necessity. Christ does not just open the door of opportunity. He extends His hand and helps us through it.

—BRAD WILCOX

The atonement of the Son of God is a principle that should be clearly understood by us, because unless there is an intelligent comprehension of it, we fail to appreciate the value of the salvation that has been extended to us through the atonement of our Redeemer. It is a great mystery to many people that Christ should die and that through His death redemption should come; and because it is a mystery and they cannot comprehend it by their human wisdom, they are inclined to reject Him as their Savior.

—GEORGE Q. CANNON

Some happy endings will never be read in this life. But the atonement of Jesus Christ promises us that our stories will all have successful conclusions one day, if we put our trust in him. He who sees the end from the beginning and desires above all for us to enjoy immortality and eternal life will lead us to our own "happily ever afters," if we will follow in his ways. Things may not always make sense. Gates may be closed to us for a time. And trials may assail us. But if we can be enduring to the end, all these things will work for our good, and we will find ourselves as polished gems in the hands of our Maker.

—Emily Watts

And he was withdrawn from them
about a stone's cast,
and kneeled down, and prayed,
Saying, Father, if thou be willing,
remove this cup from me:
nevertheless not my will,
but thine, be done.
And there appeared an angel
unto him from heaven,
strengthening him.

—LUKE 21:41–43

If we visualize the image of the bitter cup we come to understand its symbolic power. When we drink something very bitter the body naturally shakes or trembles. If you were to drink a glass of strong vinegar or something equally bitter, your body would react instantly. . . . It is a natural response. That is the image of the Savior which he used himself during his atoning hour. He spoke of that cup in his prayer from Gethsemane. He used the image of the cup in his deepest, most earnest moment (see Luke 22:44), when he pleaded in Gethsemane with his Father.

—S. MICHAEL WILCOX

When I was pregnant with my last daughter, Grace, I began to experience complications. I went into preterm labor at seventeen weeks and spent six months down flat in bed, only getting up once a week to go to the doctor. Because of the severe restrictions placed upon me, I could not attend church for those six months. During that time the Young Men in our ward brought the sacrament into my home.

There, in my living room, they would kneel beside my sofa table, which had been draped with a white linen cloth. On that table they carefully placed *one* piece of bread and *one* cup of water. In that moment it became clear to me how individual the Atonement really is. *I* was the brokenhearted. *I* was the one held captive. *I* was the one seeking comfort. He was *my* Savior, *my* Messiah. . . . I was in His hands.

—Emily Freeman

What a devastating blow to death when Christ first unlocked the doors to the masses of imprisoned spirits who had so awaited the day of his triumphant resurrection! He arose from the grave "with healing in his wings" (2 Nephi 25:13) for all men. He opened the door that had been shut for thousands of years on billions of graves. He was the first to walk through that door, and then, in a display of unequaled mercy, he left it open for others to exit in a divinely determined sequence.

—TAD R. CALLISTER

Adam, after he was cast out of the garden, was commanded to offer sacrifices to God; by this act, he and all who participated in the offerings of sacrifices, were reminded of the Savior who should come to redeem them from death which, were it not for the atonement wrought out by him, would forever exclude them from dwelling in the presence of God again.

—Joseph F. Smith

Gethsemane was the place where he renewed and deepened his internal commitment, or covenant, with his Father to complete his atoning mission. . . . Christ's Calvary was successful partly because his Gethsemane was successful. . . . He fought and conquered the central issue that fractures most people's lives: my will versus thy will. Jesus decided, he pledged, he promised, he covenanted with God, "Thy will be done."

—STEPHEN R. COVEY

The Lord Jesus Christ had experienced, first-hand, treachery of the vilest degree. On the day of His trial, an Apostle and a witness of Him turned traitor. Enemies had stalked this man who shunned violence, who never cursed or lifted His voice or hand, who ate with sinners and the poor as well as those recognized as important. Finally, those on the errand of the evil one took him prisoner. They subjected him to a mock trial and crowned His head with thorns; they made a mockery of justice. He stood silent, knowing of a far greater plan than his trumped-up crucifixion. They paraded Him through Jerusalem; they condemned Him to hang on a cross, among thieves.

Yet, He was calm. His Father's ways were His ways. He intended to fulfill His Father's plan because He knew, with Godlike knowledge, that charity never faileth.

—HEIDI S. SWINTON

If men are to be freed from the results of their own transgressions and brought back into the presence of God, they must be the beneficiaries of some expedient beyond themselves which will free them from the effect of their own sins. For this purpose was the atonement of Jesus Christ conceived and executed.

This was the world's supreme act of charity, performed by Jesus out of his great love for us. He not only thereby met the demands of the law of justice—which would have left us forever marred by the effects of our own transgressions—but made effective the law of mercy, through which all men may be cleansed from their own sins.

—MARION G. ROMNEY

It is almost incomprehensible to think that finite, imperfect, wicked men would take a member of the Godhead—an individual who had created galaxies, solar systems, and planets, who had only to speak and have worlds come into existence—and judge him to be of no worth, a cipher, a nothing. Knowing as we do what power lay at his disposal, it is an incredible thing to consider what he endured during those fateful few hours of his atonement and crucifixion. . . . He endured it quietly because of his love for us—surely an act of astonishing condescension.

—GERALD N. LUND

All nature shrinks from death, and there is a physical horror of the separation between body and soul which, as a purely natural phenomenon, is in every instance only *overcome,* and that only by a higher principle. And we conceive that the purer the being the greater the violence of the tearing asunder of the bond with which God Almighty originally bound together body and soul. In the Perfect Man this must have reached the highest degree.

—ALFRED EDERSHEIM

It is only by and through His word that true light and knowledge are revealed, only through His name that our prayers are heard. It is by and through His name and word that we can stand in holy places, that our sick are healed, our families protected, our wounds salved, and our spirits lifted. It is only by becoming like Him that our problems can hope to find solution. It is only through His atonement we are saved.

—BEVERLY CAMPBELL

It was in Gethsemane where Jesus took on Himself the sins of the world, in Gethsemane where His pain was equivalent to the cumulative burden of all men, in Gethsemane where He descended below all things so that all could repent and come to Him. The mortal mind fails to fathom, the tongue cannot express, the pen of man cannot describe the breadth, the depth, or height of the suffering of our Lord—nor His infinite love for us.

—Ezra Taft Benson

When Jesus came, He came as a sacrifice not simply in the interest of Israel, or the posterity of Abraham, Isaac and Jacob, but in the interest of the whole human family, that in Him all men might be blessed, that in Him all men might be saved; and His mission was to make provision by which the whole human family might receive the benefits of the everlasting Gospel, not, as I say, Israel alone, but the whole human race; and not alone those dwelling upon the earth, but those also in the spirit world.

—LORENZO SNOW

Though all of Jesus' miracles testify of his divinity, most were performed because he felt profound compassion and love for each person who was blessed by his hand. . . . His love included not only the transcendent act of laying down his life for the world but also countless small acts of kindness for individuals, not only saving men from death and hell but also compassionately saving them suffering and pain.

—BRENT L. TOP

We cannot comprehend the great suffering that the Lord had to take upon himself to bring to pass this redemption from death and from sin. . . . We get into the habit of thinking, I suppose, that his great suffering was when he was nailed to the cross by his hands and his feet and was left there to suffer until he died. As excruciating as that pain was, that was not the greatest suffering that he had to undergo, for in some way which I cannot understand, but which I accept on faith, and which you must accept on faith, he carried on his back the burden of the sins of the whole world. It is hard enough for me to carry my own sins. How is it with you? And yet he had to carry the sins of the whole world, as our Savior and the Redeemer of a fallen world, and so great was his suffering before he ever went to the cross, we are informed, that blood oozed from the pores of his body.

—JOSEPH FIELDING SMITH

The only thing that provides real lifting—lifting beyond mortality and all of its chaos and troubles, beyond our own weaknesses and sins and changing fortunes, beyond our own pain and suffering and success—the only real lifting comes through our Savior and Redeemer, Jesus Christ.

—Virginia H. Pearce

The moment the atonement of the Savior is done away, that moment, at one sweep, the hopes of salvation entertained by the Christian world are destroyed, the foundation of their faith is taken away, and there is nothing left for them to stand upon. When it is gone all the revelations God ever gave to the Jewish nation, to the Gentiles, and to us are rendered valueless, and all hope is taken from us at one sweep.

—BRIGHAM YOUNG

The power of the Atonement is not limited to knowledge alone. The Atonement also provides power to do. . . . And when we fail, it is the power to try again. Faith of sufficient intensity will always lead to repentance. We apply the Atonement when we have "faith unto repentance" (Alma 34:15).

—BRAD WILCOX

The powers in the Atonement apply to our lives right now and are accessible to you and me right now. These powers have implications for every relationship we have and in every combination of people we find ourselves with. They have implications for what we think and say, what we do, and how we feel. These powers may hold the secret to making right relationships endure and may help us to know what is wrong with potentially good relationships that are going wrong.

—M. CATHERINE THOMAS

We must always remember that the Atonement of Jesus Christ was a foreordained assignment by our Heavenly Father to redeem his children after their fallen state. It was an act of love by our Heavenly Father to permit his Only Begotten to make an atoning sacrifice. And it was a supreme act of love by his beloved Son to carry out the Atonement.

—HOWARD W. HUNTER

NOVEMBER

~

Once he groaned in blood and tears;
Now in glory he appears.
Once rejected by his own,
Now their King he shall be known.

—Parley P. Pratt

There is no flesh
that can dwell in the presence of God,
save it be through the merits,
and mercy,
and grace of the Holy Messiah,
who layeth down his life
according to the flesh,
and taketh it again
by the power of the Spirit,
that he may bring to pass
the resurrection of the dead,
being the first that should rise.

—2 NEPHI 2:8

For John, what at first seems a simple story—Jesus is arrested, sentenced, and executed as a result of a conspiracy to kill him—really turns out to be exactly the opposite. He is not arrested in the ordinary sense of the word, but he gives himself up to his captors. While his enemies mock, scourge, and crucify him, Jesus turns out not to be the victim but the King of Israel. The passion and the resurrection became the first steps back to glory, where he was in the beginning (see John 1:1–5).

—RICHARD NEITZEL HOLZAPFEL

We want it distinctly understood that we believe absolutely in Jesus Christ, that He was the Son of God, and that He did come to the earth with a divinely appointed mission to die on the cross as the Redeemer of mankind. We do not believe that He was just a "great moral teacher," but that He is our Redeemer.

—HEBER J. GRANT

Christ's Atonement, of course, is for super sinners and the midrange sinners and then good people who make a lot of mistakes but are not wicked! Each of these acts of drawing upon the Atonement requires us to put off the natural man. I am persuaded that so much of taking up the cross daily—daily, not quarterly or semiannually—consists of putting off the natural man (see Mosiah 3:19).

—NEAL A. MAXWELL

Misfortune and hardship lose their tragedy when viewed through the lens of the Atonement. The process could be explained this way: The more we know the Savior, the longer becomes our view. The more we see His truths, the more we feel His joy. But it is one thing to know that's the right answer in a Sunday School class and quite another to experience firsthand a cheerful outlook when current circumstances are far from what we hoped. If we would develop faith to apply the Atonement in this manner and not merely talk about it, awareness of imaginary finite boundaries inadvertently placed on the Savior's infinite sacrifice can be meaningful. Consider two false assumptions that, if pursued, will block our appreciation and access to the Lord's divine assistance.

False assumption 1—We can avoid tribulation.

False assumption 2—We can trust in our own efforts.

—CAMILLE FRONK OLSON

If we would have God "apply the atoning blood of Christ" (Mosiah 4:2) to our case, we can also reject it. We can take advantage of it, or we can refuse it. The Atonement is either dead to us or in full effect. It is the supreme sacrifice made for us, and to receive it, we must live up to every promise and covenant related to it. . . . We cannot enjoy optional obedience to the laws of God, or place our own limits on the law of sacrifice, or mitigate the charges of righteous conduct connected with living the gospel. We cannot be willing to sacrifice only that which is convenient to part with, and then expect a reward. The Atonement is everything; it is not to be had "on the cheap."

—HUGH W. NIBLEY

The Savior came and tabernacled in the flesh, and entered upon the duties of the priesthood at 30 years of age. After laboring three and a half years He was crucified and put to death in fulfillment of certain predictions concerning him. He laid down his life as a sacrifice for sin, to redeem the world. When men are called upon to repent of their sins, the call has reference to their own individual sins, not to Adam's transgressions. What is called the original sin was atoned for through the death of Christ irrespective of any action on the part of man; also man's individual sin was atoned for by the same sacrifice, but on condition of his obedience to the Gospel plan of salvation when proclaimed in his hearing.

—WILFORD WOODRUFF

Luke, who tradition says was a physician, recorded that great drops of blood came from the Savior's pores (Luke 22:44). The bitterness oozed. It is not a spectacle one wishes to recall, but we have been commanded, and weekly we memorialize it in an ordinance called the sacrament. Even then, all His preparation and all that He could summon from His own strength was not sufficient. And more earnestly, says the record, He prayed, and an angel came, strengthening Him (see Luke 22:34–44). Strengthening, but not delivering. What is it like to have the power to summon legions of angels to end the ordeal yet not to summon them?

—TRUMAN G. MADSEN

Over my years, I have been called and tried to comfort those who mourn, but until I had to repeat those very things to myself that I have been saying to others, then only did I come to sense something that was far beyond words, that had to reach down to the touchstone of the soul. . . . You have to see the loved one die and then you have to ask yourself—Do you believe what you have been teaching others? Are you sure and certain that God lives? Do you believe in the Atonement of the Lord and Master—that He opened the doors to the resurrection in the more glorious life? Sometimes when we stand in the stark nakedness all alone, it's then that our testimony has to grow deep if we are not going to be shattered and fall by the wayside.

—HAROLD B. LEE

Can any of us, in any possible way, begin to comprehend even in the smallest part what it meant for God the Father to send his Son on his mission to earth, knowing what must come to pass if he were to finish the work he volunteered to do? And how could the Son, even the Son of God, say to the Father, "Thy will be done," knowing what would be required?

—ARDETH GREENE KAPP

Christ gave His life willingly and voluntarily for the redemption of mankind. He had offered Himself, in the primeval council in heaven, as the subject of the atoning sacrifice made necessary by the foreseen transgression of the first man; and the free agency shown and exercised in this, the early stage of His saving mission, was retained to the very last of the agonizing fulfilment of the accepted plan....

The motive inspiring and sustaining Him through all the scenes of His mission, from the time of His primeval ordination to the moment of victorious consummation on the cross, was twofold: first, the desire to do His Father's will in accomplishing the redemption of mankind; second, His love for humanity, of whose welfare and destiny He had assumed charge.

—JAMES E. TALMAGE

Infinite literally means "not finite" or "not finished," and synonyms of *infinite* include endless, limitless, boundless, and eternal. Thus, passages that describe the atonement as infinite imply that the atonement is not bound to a single sphere or space, such as our earth, solar system, or universe, but rather that it is infinite in its scope. The atonement is not limited to a specific number of God's children; it reaches through time retrospectively (backward in time) and prospectively (forward in time) and blesses all of God's children regardless of when they experienced or will experience mortality. The atonement is not limited to God's children—all of his creations benefit from the atonement, including creatures (fish, fowl, animals), earths, and more.

—DONALD W. PARRY AND JAY A. PARRY

Perhaps as we reflect on our lives, it is easy to convince ourselves we have sinned too often and gone too far to deserve the Atonement. We criticize ourselves harshly and beat ourselves up mercilessly. Perhaps we feel we have stepped beyond the reach of the Atonement by knowingly repeating a previously forsaken sin. We understand that God and Jesus were willing to forgive the first time, but we wonder how many more times they will be willing to watch us bumble along before they finally roll their eyes and declare, "Enough already!" We struggle so much to forgive ourselves that we wrongly assume God must be having the same struggle. . . . When we're tempted to give up, we must remember God is long-suffering, change is a process, and repentance is a pattern in our lives.

—BRAD WILCOX

While even the unbeliever must see what the life and death of Jesus have effected in the world, to the believer that life and death are something deeper still; to him they are nothing less than a resurrection from the dead. He sees in the cross of Christ something which far transcends its historical significance. He sees in it the fulfilment of all prophecy as well as the consummation of all history; he sees in it the explanation of the mystery of birth, and the conquest over the mystery of the grave. In that life he finds a perfect example; in that death an infinite redemption.

—FREDERIC FARRAR

Can we comprehend what it might be like to be invited to sit on the right hand of God at some future day because we truly fed the hungry, clothed the naked, visited the sick, and administered to their relief, "both spiritually and temporally, according to their wants" (see Matthew 25:34–40; Mosiah 4:26)? May our awareness of the Savior and those for whom He suffered and died cause us to be willing to serve Him by serving others. May we come unto Jesus with broken hearts and contrite spirits, ready to participate in the needed miracles.

—MARY ELLEN EDMUNDS

When Jesus was raised from the dead He became the first fruits of the resurrection. The spirit begotten of the Father (the intelligent part of His soul) reinhabited His earthly tabernacle which had been purified, and He became a glorified celestial being, and took His place, on the right hand of the Father, as one of the Godhead. He had power to overcome death because He had complied with all the laws of His Father governing it; and having subdued death He turned the key whereby all mankind may be resurrected, and all may be glorified also by obeying His teachings, which are so simple that all may comply if they will.

—George Albert Smith

It is not God's will for us to stoically "go down with the ship" when rescuers are all around. I believe that the ability to say "I am hurting and need help" is a humble and courageous act of meekness. Even Christ, when he was in agony, pleaded with his disciples to stay with him and pray with him, as he himself "prayed more earnestly" to his Father (Luke 22:44). If God himself can ask for help from friends, family, and priesthood leaders, undoubtedly we will not make it through life without doing the same.

—Patricia T. Holland

My good works are necessary, but they are not sufficient. I cannot work myself into celestial glory, and I cannot guarantee myself a place among the sanctified through my own unaided efforts. Therefore, even though my own merits are essential to salvation, they alone will not take me where I need to go. Rather, it is by and through the merits of Christ. This transcendent truth should create, not feelings of futility, but feelings of deep humility.

—ROBERT L. MILLET

In Gethsemane, on that terrible but glorious night, in a scene so personal as almost to dissuade us from listening in, Jesus cried out in shockingly familiar tones, "Daddy (Papa), all things are possible for you. Please take this experience away—it is worse than even I thought it would be. Nevertheless, I will do what you desire and not what I desire."

It is important to remember that this plea was not theatrics. This petition really happened between a son and his father. It is a privileged communication, but we have been extended the privilege of learning about it because of God's love for us and his trust that we will hold it in reverence.

—ANDREW C. SKINNER

No matter how lost the world at large may be, no matter how depraved or degenerate it may become, there is yet a bright light of hope for those individuals who have a faith in Christ. Those who focus on him and his atoning sacrifice, who let these glorious truths rest in their minds continually, will find that Christ's power to lift the human soul transcends even the weightiest burdens the world may thrust upon them.

—TAD R. CALLISTER

Jesus is the Christ, our Redeemer and Savior and King. His Atonement is filled with both redeeming and enabling power. Because He came and did what He was sent to do, because He bore the weight of all the sin and pain of the world, we have access to divine power to help us deal with challenges we could never handle on our own, to find the peace that passeth understanding even in anxious, heartbreaking times.

—SHERI DEW

Behold, I am Jesus Christ,
whom the prophets testified
shall come into the world.
And behold, I am the light
and the life of the world;
and I have drunk out of that bitter cup
which the Father hath given me,
and have glorified the Father
in taking upon me the sins of the world,
in the which I have suffered
the will of the Father
in all things from the beginning.

—3 Nephi 11:10–11

What does it mean to keep the faith? It means first, that we accept Jesus Christ, not merely as a great teacher, a powerful leader, but as the Savior, the Redeemer of the world. . . . I would have all men keep that faith. I think it is fundamental to man's happiness, fundamental to his peace of mind. I think it is the cardinal principle of the Church of Jesus Christ.

—DAVID O. McKAY

[A friend of mine] wondered what she could do to comfort a neighbor whose son had been killed in a motorcycle accident. The neighbor was not an active church member and [my friend] was anxious to help but didn't know what to do. She offered a prayer that she could bring some solace, and went without anything in her hands. In her visit she felt impressed to bear her testimony of the Atonement and the opportunity to live with a loving Heavenly Father. That assurance was just what the neighbor needed. She said, "I have prayed to know where my son was. Nobody has ever told me. That's what I needed to hear."

—ELAINE L. JACK

Just as we cannot understand in mortality how the Resurrection is made possible, neither do we know why or how Christ "pays" for our sins. But there is plenty that we do understand: the nature of sin, its destructive consequences, our need to repent, and the assurance of forgiveness if we do. We can be grateful for Christ's grace, which, indeed, is "sufficient" (2 Corinthians 12:9) both for overcoming death on our behalf and, united with our best efforts, for overcoming ignorance and sin within us.

—LOWELL L. BENNION

Whenever I have visited Gethsemane in the Holy Land, the great emotion I feel there is one of gratitude—my gratitude for him certainly, but also a more profound gratitude, the gratitude of the Savior to his Father in Heaven for allowing him to take our pains that we would not, as he says in Doctrine and Covenants 19, need to suffer them (see D&C 19:16). So to me, amidst the groundswell of mercy which permeates Gethsemane, it is also the place of deepest gratitude on earth. The experiences the Savior had there intensified his forgiving nature, refining the already eternal refinement he brought with him to that stable of Bethlehem. Throughout his life and ministry he demonstrated that forgiveness, as if he knew we'd need constant encouragement in our need for constant mercy.

—S. Michael Wilcox

Returning means coming full circle to the place where we began. Returning to the presence of our loving Heavenly Father has always been my desire. In another sense, *returning* can mean turning around, getting on the right course, or admitting a mistake. The Atonement of Jesus Christ makes it possible for those who have strayed from the path to repent and return.

—Elaine S. Dalton

How glorious is the resurrection (planned from before the foundation of the world) of the Christ, designated in some scriptures, even as of that time, as the Lamb of God. I cannot comprehend what the resurrection did. I have read nothing that explains to my mind what the resurrection, biologically or physiologically, is. I feel quite convinced that if it were explained, that it would be in language and invoking principles that I would not understand. The Lord has given us all that we need to know—that Christ is our Savior, the Redeemer of the world, the One through whom we attain that destiny which is marked out as possible for all of God's children who earn it.

Eternal progression is brought about through that Atonement. We may go on and on forever. That is our destiny through the Atonement of Jesus Christ.

—J. REUBEN CLARK JR.

You and I do not have to lift our burdens alone. In fact, we should not. Christ performed the miraculous Atonement to assist all of us. When we do not plead for the grace of Christ to assist us, we only hurt ourselves and miss out on what could be a holy place. I encourage you to seek the gift of grace. Christ will give you power to do the things in your life that seem beyond your capacity. Turn to Him for the help you need, and He will give you His "divine means of help" (Bible Dictionary, "Grace").

—Kris Belcher

The Atonement guarantees all will survive mortality, but growth is optional. Christ is not forcing progress on us, nor can He change us against our wills. We have the right to accept or reject His offering. We can acknowledge and appreciate it or ridicule and despise it, but we can't fault Christ for giving us the opportunity to reach our potential.

—BRAD WILCOX

DECEMBER

～

He left his Father's courts on high,
With man to live, for man to die,
A world to purchase and to save
And seal a triumph o'er the grave.

—ELIZA R. SNOW

Jesus perfected his life and became our Christ. Priceless blood of a god was shed, and he became our Savior; his perfected life was given, and he became our Redeemer; his atonement for us made possible our return to our Heavenly Father, and yet how thoughtless, how unappreciative are most beneficiaries! Ingratitude is a sin of the ages.

—Spencer W. Kimball

Jesus knows that when we sin, we are selling ourselves for nothing because we have not understood our worth. Yet we are actually of such great value that there could never be enough money to buy us back from sin. Only the priceless blood of Jesus could do it. And he spent it all for us. He speaks to us across two thousand years by his sacrifice, his obedience, and his complete consecration to our Father that we may learn to rely "alone upon the merits of Christ, who was the author and the finisher of [our] faith" (Moroni 6:4).

—ANN N. MADSEN

It is to many a matter of surpassing wonder that the voluntary sacrifice of a single being could be made to operate as a means of ransom for the rest of mankind. In this, as in other things, the scriptures are explicable by the spirit of scriptural interpretation. The sacred writings of ancient times, the inspired utterances of latter-day prophets, the traditions of mankind, the rites of sacrifice, and even the sacrileges of heathen idolatries, all involve the idea of vicarious atonement. God has never refused to accept an offering made by one who is authorized on behalf of those who are in any way incapable of doing the required service themselves.

—James E. Talmage

The scriptures contain more accounts of Jesus healing the sick than of any other kind of miracle. Christ's power over all manner of afflictions, diseases, and infirmities not only manifests the Savior's perfect love and compassion for people but also typifies the transcendent healing his atoning sacrifice affords us.

—BRENT L. TOP

How grateful we are for the privilege of praying in the name of the Savior—in the name of the boy who played in the streets of Nazareth and understands this mortal life completely, in the name of the one who sacrificed Himself that we might live again with Him and the Father, who are the ultimate sources of comfort and peace.

—Marjorie Pay Hinckley

They came out with sword and with staves to capture the man of peace, the man who forbade violence, who had never lifted His voice nor His hand against the innocent and the good, nor indeed against any man, except only against their wicked practices and evil-doings—they came out to take Him prisoner and to pass Him through a mock trial, that they might find occasion to condemn Him to death. . . . In the midst of His trial, when mocked, when smitten, when crowned with thorns, and when reviled against, he reviled not again, but meekly submitted to His lot and suffered that which God permitted the wicked to inflict upon Him. He was brought into circumstances where the doctrine He taught could be put to the test, and in all He proved the genuineness of His teaching.

—JOSEPH F. SMITH

It is not necessary for anyone to depend continually upon the testimony of another person regarding the mediation, atonement, and resurrection of Christ as our Redeemer and Savior. Each can savor the sweetness of the truths of the gospel by obedience to the principles, ordinances, and covenants. One can still go to the Garden of Gethsemane, but the Lord Jesus cannot be found there, nor is he in the Garden Tomb. He is not on the road to Emmaus, nor in Galilee, nor at Nazareth or Bethlehem. He must be found in one's heart. But he left us the great Comforter (John 14:16) and the everlasting power of the priesthood.

—JAMES E. FAUST

The Savior went all the way, through the agony of the Garden of Gethsemane, taking upon himself the sins of the world, to the cross where even in the last moment of his suffering, he prayed for his crucifiers. He died on the cross. He gave his life for us. Yes, this is what he did for you and for me. Is it asking too much for us to press forward with steadfastness? All the way? Every day?

—ARDETH GREENE KAPP

As for submissiveness, it is both proper and important for us in our afflictions and trials to ask for relief through fasting, prayer, and priesthood blessings. But after all we can do, we then submit to God's will as did Jesus in Gethsemane and on the cross, when, in anguish, He posed aloud the possibility that the cup might pass from Him. On that occasion, the key word that expressed Jesus' attribute of submissiveness was "nevertheless."

—NEAL A. MAXWELL

The Atonement does more than pay for our sins. It is also the agent through which we develop a saintly nature. When the Savior accepts our repentance and pours down charity, His pure love, He restores our spiritual balance.

—HEIDI S. SWINTON

The totality of human pain cannot fit within the bounds of the human heart; it could find place only in the heart of the Atoning Son, and it caused even him to tremble and shrink. . . . When we speak of human suffering, we must realize that only Christ has experienced that totality; we have experienced merely our own petitions of "Abba, Father, all things are possible unto thee; take away this cup from me" (Mark 14:36).

—S. MICHAEL WILCOX

Listen to him who is the advocate
with the Father,
who is pleading your cause before him—
Saying: Father, behold the sufferings and death
of him who did no sin,
in whom thou wast well pleased;
behold the blood of thy Son which was shed,
the blood of him whom thou gavest
that thyself might be glorified;
Wherefore, Father, spare these my brethren
that believe on my name,
that they may come unto me
and have everlasting life.

—D&C 45:3–5

God never bestows upon His people, or upon an individual, superior blessings without a severe trial to prove them, to prove that individual, or that people, to see whether they will keep their covenants with Him, and keep in remembrance what He has shown them. . . . For this express purpose the Father withdrew His spirit from His son, at the time he was to be crucified. . . . The light, knowledge, power, and glory with which he was clothed were far above, or exceeded that of all others who had been upon the earth after the fall, consequently at the very moment, at the hour when the crisis came for him to offer up his life, the Father withdrew Himself, withdrew His Spirit, and cast a vail over him.

—BRIGHAM YOUNG

As I anticipate seeing the Savior, I . . . think more deeply about what he did for me in a very personal way in the Garden, such that he can understand everything—everything we feel, everything we experience, everything that makes us feel lonely and heavily burdened. He knows. He understands. He's been there. He loved us that much then, and oh, how he loves us right now. There is nothing we can do to cause him to stop loving us. Nothing. And just because I don't understand unconditional love doesn't make it unreal. It is real. God loves us, the Savior loves us—they love us unconditionally. They love us right now.

—MARY ELLEN EDMUNDS

Like many words, *redeemer* has multiple meanings. Customary definitions include one who buys or wins back; one who frees us from captivity or debt by the payment of ransom; one who returns or restores. However, in recent years I have come to appreciate an additional dictionary definition that adds significance to all others: A redeemer is one who changes us for the better, one who reforms and reshapes us. The Atonement of Jesus Christ buys us back, frees us from captivity, and returns us to God, but it also offers us much more than a grand reunion with our Heavenly Parents. Being recovered, rescued, reconciled, reunited, and reinstated would all ultimately be disappointing if we could not also be renewed. . . . Redemption is more than paying justice and bringing everyone back to God. It is mercifully giving us the opportunity of being comfortable there. Not only can we go home, we can also feel at home.

—BRAD WILCOX

We should continue to stress the importance of faith, of repentance, of obedience and strive with all our hearts to be full of faith and demonstrate good works in our lives. But we should never lose sight of the great overriding fact of the grace of our Lord and Savior and the wholly *central* part it plays in our atonement and salvation.

—GERALD N. LUND

There is no such thing as a "magic formula" which, when followed, eliminates problems, stresses, and hard times. Even Christ, in his agony in the Garden of Gethsemane, prayed unto the Father that, if it was possible, "let this cup pass from me." He then added an important qualifying phrase: "Nevertheless not my will, but thine, be done." (Luke 22:42; see also Matthew 26:39; Mark 14:36.) In this case the cup was not, and could not be, removed. Nevertheless, the Father came to the aid of his Only Begotten Son: "And there appeared an angel unto him from heaven, strengthening him." (Luke 22:43.)

Having been *strengthened,* Jesus Christ went forth to accomplish his foreordained mission—the ultimate sacrifice, the great Atonement.

—Carolyn J. Rasmus

I bear witness that Jesus is the Messiah and that He could not have known, according to the flesh, how to succor His people according to their infirmities unless He had gone through in Gethsemane what He went through. I bear testimony that the knowledge He has today, what one of the prophets calls "the bowels of mercy," reaches out unto the Father, who grieves that any tree in His vineyard should be lost. He pleads even now for more time, for you and for me, until we too have been purged and can sing the song of redeeming love.

—TRUMAN G. MADSEN

There are two great gifts that come through the atonement of Jesus Christ. The resurrection of the dead—the defeat of Satan and death, and the restoration of every creature born into this world to life. That is a gift that comes without their asking for it. It is one they cannot refuse to receive. It is not one that they receive by merit. It is a free gift. It comes to both good and bad alike; not one soul will fail of the resurrection. If one did, Christ would not gain the victory and so he redeems every soul from a condition for which they were not responsible. On the other hand, He died to redeem only those who are willing to obey His commandments and walk humbly in the light of truth from their own sins. Every man will pay a price for his own sins who will not repent and accept Jesus Christ and keep his commandments, the gospel of Jesus Christ.

—Joseph Fielding Smith

As life supplies its store of tribulation we need the consolation that comes with knowing that God is good and that he is near, that he understands, and that he loves us and will help us and strengthen us for the realities of a world where sin and affliction exist....

From this source—from God and Christ—wisdom and strength can be found that will make endurance possible, and relationships generous and helpful, that will lead to abundancy of life and to everlasting life.

—Marion D. Hanks

The Atonement was plainly to be a vicarious sacrifice, voluntary and love-inspired on the Savior's part, universal in its application to mankind so far as men shall accept the means of deliverance thus placed within their reach. For such a mission only one who was without sin could be eligible. Even the altar victims of ancient Israel offered as a provisional propitiation for the offenses of the people under the Mosaic law had to be clean and devoid of spot or blemish; otherwise they were unacceptable and the attempt to offer them was sacrilege. Jesus Christ was the only Being suited to the requirements of the great sacrifice.

—JAMES E. TALMAGE

For me, the Lord's prayer, "Give us this day our daily bread" (Matthew 6:11) doesn't just refer to the physical food necessary to get through the day. It means "give me this day Christ, the bread of life, give me his atonement, so that this day I might turn the other cheek, I might go the second mile, I might feel to forgive as he forgave the Roman soldiers while he hung on the cross.

—STEPHEN R. COVEY

The fundamental principles of our religion are the testimony of the Apostles and Prophets, concerning Jesus Christ, that He died, was buried, and rose again the third day, and ascended into heaven; and all other things which pertain to our religion are only appendages to it.

—JOSEPH SMITH

All that we have to give back to God at the end of our lives is our characters. If we have spent our lives living a lie or being one person on the outside but another person on the inside, then we have taken the Savior's gift of complete atonement and perfect love and have given him a flawed gift in return, not a whole heart that can be healed and sanctified.

—CHIEKO OKAZAKI

The life of Jesus Christ, born in a stable, cradled in a manger and put to death between two thieves, was one of the greatest of all failures from man's point of view, but our Lord and Master came to the earth not to do His own will but that of His Father, and He successfully fulfilled His mission. He has triumphed over death, hell and the grave and has earned the reward of a throne at the right hand of His Father.

—HEBER J. GRANT

A dead Christ might have been a Teacher and Wonder-worker, and remembered and loved as such. But only a Risen and Living Christ could be the Saviour, the Life, and the Life-Giver—and as such preached to all men. And of this most blessed truth we have the fullest and most unquestionable evidence.

—ALFRED EDERSHEIM

The will of the Son was fully swallowed up in the will of the Father. The unparalleled prayer and desire of the Savior articulated in Gethsemane—"thy will be done"—was now fulfilled in every way, completely satisfying every aim, goal, purpose, and requirement of the plan of salvation. That is, in actuality, the sense of the Greek verb used in John's account of Jesus' sixth statement: "It is *finished*" (John 19:30; emphasis added). The verb translated into English as "finished" is *tetelestai* (from *teleo*), which means "to fulfill something, to make something complete." That is what Golgotha did. That which was started in Gethsemane was completed at Golgotha.

—Andrew C. Skinner

He suffered himself to be lifted up upon the cross that we might be lifted up, back to our Father, clothed with immortality and eternal life. And our part is easy, as simple in design as the Egyptian ankh. In faith, each of us takes the only thing we really have—our agency—and offers it back to him joyfully, voluntarily, and quietly.

—VIRGINIA H. PEARCE

It seems that some people lose sight and hope of godhood, not because of major sins, but because of innocent mistakes or weaknesses. "I'm not a bad person," they say. "I just can't seem to overcome the weaknesses that so easily beset me and distance me from God. It's not the sins so much as the lack of talent, the lack of capability, the lack of strength that separate me from God." Those of us who fall within this category need to be reminded of the Atonement's intimate, as well as infinite reach. Regardless of the depth or multiplicity of our individual weaknesses, the Atonement is always there. Therein lies its beauty and genius—it is never beyond our grasp. The Savior is always standing by, anxiously longing to endow us with those powers that will convert our every weakness to a strength.

—TAD R. CALLISTER

We may be on the strait and narrow, but how is our pace? We may be holding to the iron rod, but how tight is our grip? . . .

In the context of the Atonement of Christ, failure is not a problem. Mediocrity is not a problem. Even immaturity, insecurity, and fear are not problems. Complacency is a problem. Indifference is a problem.

—BRAD WILCOX

He will swallow up death in victory;
and the Lord God
will wipe away tears from off all faces;
and the rebuke of his people
shall he take away
from off all the earth:
for the Lord hath spoken it.

—Isaiah 25:8

IMAGE CREDITS